WHAT PEOPLE ARE SAYING ABOUT *JOHN CALVIN'S GENEVA CATECHISM*

"For some church traditions, old catechisms seem like relics from a bygone era. And yet, if we engage timeless catechisms like Calvin's, we see that chewing on and digesting rich theology is always nurturing to our souls. I'm thankful that Joshua Torrey took up the mantle to provide this beautiful resource to a new generation of Christians."

— BRANDON D. SMITH, AUTHOR OF *ROOTED* AND *ECHOES OF THE REFORMATION*

"I could not be more joyous that there is an effort in place to republish it, that it might find a wider audience. I fully intend to utilize the catechism in leading my son in the faith, as well as sharing much of its treasure with any who will listen."

— HANS SAUNDERS, FELLOWSHIP BIBLE NWA LAYMEN

JOHN CALVIN'S
Geneva Catechism

edited by
JOSHUA TORREY

GRACE FOR SINNERS BOOKS

ISBN-13:978-0692863237
ISBN-10: 0692863230

Cover Design by Mathew B. Sims
MathewBryanSims.com

To the one in the presence of the Lord.

"The Lord has certainly inflicted a severe and bitter wound in the death of our infant son. But he is himself a Father, and knows best what is good for his children."
— John Calvin, Letters

CONTENTS

INTRODUCTION

No name is more synonymous with Reformed Theology than John Calvin. The giant of systematic theology forever altered how theology would be performed and books written. His systematic writings, exemplified by the colossal Institutes of the Christian Religion, have impacted every subsequent theology. The preservation of his commentary on the Scriptures remain a valuable resource. His theology is devotional in its praise of God. It stands within reason to say that Calvin was a history altering theologian and pastor.

Calvin hasn't done too poorly in the modern, internet age either. His soteriological teaching has been branded with his name (Calvinism), acrostics (TULIP), and emphatic declarations (the doctrines of grace). Reformed Theology has risen to fame, even in secular communities, off of the ground breaking work of John Calvin.

My own introduction to the writing of John Calvin came at the hands of his Institutes of the Christian Religion. Nearing the end of my studies in engineering, a copy was gifted as a graduation present. Being a veracious reader, I knew nothing else but to start at the front and work my way through. My original copy still retains my original

INTRODUCTION

markings. I, a stumbling Baptist at the time, was flung upside down theologically by Calvin. I was naively shocked that Calvin's systematic thought went well beyond soteriology. Peripheral debates of Calvinism-Arminianism were rendered mute or irrelevantly shallow. In Calvin, I found a humanistic, yet biblical theology that touched on the full scope of the Christian experience—not just salvation.

My trajectory was set. To this day, I remain more "Calvin-ist" than Reformed—though I see no serious disagreements between the two. For each hour studying a Reformed creed or document, I study two hours of Calvin. Calvin as a theologian was worthy of all the attention I gave him. Reading books such as Karl Barth's *The Theology of John Calvin* and I. John Hesselink's *Calvin's First Catechism: A Commentary* only confirmed this. As this study—and my writing—increased I spent much time with Calvin's 1545 Genevan Catechism (his second attempt).

Calvin's first attempt in 1538 was a paragraph style confession that has been preserved in English by Ford Lewis Battles. However, Calvin made alterations for the education of children in a true "catechism" style only a few years later. It stands as a historical landmark in the theological output of Calvin (the third edition of his Institutes was published in 1543). Containing the almost fully developed theology of Calvin, the catechism is worthy of preservation because of its simplicity and comprehensive nature. I have relied upon it for many years now and have quoted it on many occasions to convey Calvin's thoughts in a more simple form.

The formatting that Calvin choose for the catechism is both familiar and strange. There are many questions and answers that found revision in later Reformed documents.

INTRODUCTION

But Calvin's catechism also structures its questions and answers in a more dialogue-based manner (much like Saint Anselm's Cur Deus Homo). This leaves some of the "instruction" entirely in the question itself while the answer is merely "yes" or "no." Because of this, Calvin's catechism is not particularly remarkable for memorization and has fallen out of publication. Still, the theology contained within is incredibly pertinent and accessible.

What follows in this volume is a refined version of Elijah Waterman's 1815 translation of the catechism with as few changes made as possible. Principally, only the words, format, and punctuation have been brought forward to modern vernacular and readability. My hope is that the re-publication of this catechism will bring more people into contact with the full theology of John Calvin. For all the clamor over his name, many continue to only read and apply popular portions of his thought. The thickness of his Institutes and commentaries are not found here. Hopefully, this catechism can work as a gateway to a renewed emphasis on truly Calvinistic thought.

I would like to introduce two unique and practical points that Calvin mentions very early in his catechism: Knowledge of God requires knowledge of redemption and sin rendering man as sub-human.

KNOWLEDGE OF REDEMPTION

Even if one has never read a Reformed confession, the opening question of Calvin's catechism has a familiar ring to it—"What is the chief end of man?" Across the history of the world, nations, cults, and trendy groups have attempted to answer the question of man's purpose. Peace. Prosperity. Mercy. Kindness. These are some of the most elegant

INTRODUCTION

answers. While others drinking heavily from atheistic philosophy, find cruder answers.

The question gets to the root of anthropology and theology. It speaks very specifically to the nature of man by answering with a resounding emphasis about the nature of God. The Westminster Divines apparently were familiar enough with the catechism to spot a spectacular foundation for Christian education.

In typical Calvin fashion, he answers with no subtly. Though, I do love the subtle difference of his answer compared to Westminster—"It is to know God his Creator" (Q.1). Man is created to know his creator. This principled knowing is effectual and gracious. This is not knowledge of propositions alone. It is a knowledge of God that "should advance his glory" (Q.2). As we acknowledge him as "almighty and perfectly good" (Q.9) our knowledge brings about an effect. But Calvin says this knowledge of God's perfect character is not enough.

The God of the Scriptures has revealed himself as more than pure power. He reveals his full character. And knowledge of this full character is essential for fallen man. Calvin states it like this,

10 M. Is this sufficient?
C. By no means.

11 M. Why not?
C. Because we do not deserve that he should exert his power for our assistance, or manifest his goodness for our benefit.

12 M. What more is needful?

INTRODUCTION

C. That each one of us be fully convinced that God loves him, and that he is willing to be to him a Father and a Savior.

13 M. But how will that be evident to us?
C. Truly from his word, in which he declares to us his mercy, and testifies his love for us, in Christ.

14 M. The foundation and beginning of confidence in God is then, the knowledge of him in Christ?
C. Entirely.

For fallen man, knowledge of God's might and goodness is terrifying. There is nothing in those characteristics that communicate a God who works graciously in our favor. Thus knowing and recognizing the power and authority of God is not sufficiently Christian knowledge. To know of a powerful deity is merely theism. Calvin's chief end is to know the God who "manifest his goodness for our benefit" (Q.11). It is this knowledge of God stemming from the revelation of Jesus Christ that moves to advancing the glory of God. Thus knowledge of Christ is "the foundation and beginning of confidence in God" (Q.14).

It is this knowledge of God-for-us that is the "chief good of man" (Q.3) precisely because it encourages men to glorify God. In Christ we are to "be fully convinced that God loves" us and "is willing to be ... a Father and a Savior" (Q.12). The sheer sovereignty of God is not reassuring to the heart of fallen man, but the expressed love of a Father and Savior calms all fear (1 Jn. 4:18). God reveals himself as almighty and yet merciful towards us. Similarly, God commands obedience only after he has revealed himself as the Almighty God on our behalf. God has done both of these things for the Church. He has revealed himself as the eager Father and the source of our obedient love for him (1 Jn. 4:19). It is as Calvin says, truly "living piously and justly" is nothing more than "depending upon God."

> Now, from these words, we learn for what end God gathers together for himself a church; namely, that they whom he has called, may be holy. The foundation, indeed, of the divine calling, is a gratuitous promise; but it follows immediately after, that they whom he has chosen as a peculiar people to himself, should devote themselves to the righteousness of God...Wherefore, let us know, that God manifests himself to the faithful, in order that they may live as in his sight; and may make him the arbiter not only of their works, but of their thoughts. Whence also we infer, that there is no other method of living piously and justly than that of depending upon God. – Commentary on Genesis Volume 1

In denying the God who reveals Himself (Rom 1:18-23), the world places themselves in an endless struggle to find themselves and their purpose. They are unaware that the God who reveals himself desires to be their Father and empower them to walk in glad tidings before him. This leads us to look Calvin's understanding of sin in the early section of the catechism.

ON SIN

Conceptions and definitions of "sin" have changed more than a couple times throughout church history. As with

INTRODUCTION

many church doctrines, there are a slew of (true) paradigms from which the same truth can be viewed and appreciated. One of these is the doctrine of sin.

It is certainly valuable to begin with the generic definition that sin is disobedience to God's commands. This is certainly seen in our first parents' original sin in eating the forbidden fruit. However, this definition is thin. Sin is a heart issue and not merely a mechanical outworking issue. The heart of a person matters as well as their attitude. Sin is unbelief in anything revealed by God. As Paul and the author of Hebrews elaborate, anything not done in faith is sin. These ways of understanding sin broadly describe sin in view of our relationship to God. From this paradigm, sin is principally viewed in how we are responding or interacting with God himself.

There is an additional angle that can be taken to round out our understanding of sin. This paradigm looks at sin from the perspective of God's intended purpose for man. How does sin related to man as man was meant to be? Or put another way, how can we describe sin as the deviation of man from God's purpose for him. A healthy depiction of understanding can be seen in the early portions of John Calvin's Geneva Catechism,

Q1. What is the chief end of human life?
A. To know God by whom men were created.

Q2. What reason have you for saying so?
S. Because he created us and placed us in this world to be glorified in us. And it is indeed right that our life, of which himself is the beginning, should be devoted to his glory.

INTRODUCTION

Q3. What is the highest good of man?
S. The very same thing.

Q4. Why do you hold that to be the highest good?
S. Because without it our condition is worse than that of the brutes.

Q5. Hence, then, we clearly see that nothing worse can happen to a man than not to live to God.
S. It is so.

On the basis of knowledge of God as the "chief end" for man, the glorification of God is also the goal. As the highest good, Calvin argues that the worst thing that can happen to men is that they not "live to God." This not living for God is sin. It is the withholding from God the glory that is due him (Rom. 3:23). But Calvin is not content with just this God-centric explanation.

Sin is the worst thing that happens to men and it makes them "worse than ... the brutes." The Biblical story of King Nebuchadnezzar comes to mind (Dan. 4:28-33). When man denies his "chief end," he becomes less than the creatures of the field—for they do fulfill their created purposes. The worst thing possible for man is to not fulfill his created purpose of knowing His creator. Karl Barth put it this way,

> If man misses his destination, he is inferior to the rest of creation. Not only beasts, but also stones, stars, insects, and all we see around us, leave us behind in this task of responding to the divine destination. Around us, praising is perpetual. The whole creation joins together in order to respond to God who created it. But man, in

16

INTRODUCTION

the midst of this chorus, of all this orchestration of creation, man stands still and does not do what he should do. This is man's misery: not to fulfill the meaning of his creation. – The Faith of the Church (28)

For Calvin, sin is directly linked to knowledge of God. And as such sin is not merely against God as he is, but it is also against man as God made him to be. The church must maintain that sin is always ever against God. It places us in enmity with God. It severs the relationship with our Creator. This relationship is God's purpose for man. In sin, man fights against God's purpose for himself—he becomes less than God's divine purpose. With Calvin we can say man becomes less than God designed. Or perhaps in a more extreme sense, man truly becomes less than human.

I offer these two topics as examples of Calvin's theological genius. Though many more things could be mentioned, these alone will suffice to demonstrate the value of reading Calvin's compressed and early thoughts on the full range of Christian life. Covering the knowledge of God, the Ten Commandments, and the Lord's Prayer, Calvin sets forth general guidelines on almost every important Christian doctrine.

The further study of this catechism and the elucidation of its principal truths will serve as a great encouragement to the church and the Reformed Tradition.

JOHN CALVIN'S 1554 GENEVA CATECHISM

I. THE DOCTRINES OF FAITH

Q 1. Minister, what is the chief end of man?
A. Child, it is to know God his Creator.

2 M. What reason have you for this answer?
C. Because God has created us, and placed us in this world, that he may be glorified in us. And it is certainly right, as he is the author of our life, that it should advance his glory.

3 M. What is the chief good of man?
C. It is the same thing.

4 M. Why do you account the knowledge of God to be the chief good?
C. Because without it, our condition is more miserable than that of any of the brute creatures.

5 M. From this then we clearly understand, that nothing more unhappy can befall man than not to glorify God.
C. It is so.

6 M. What is the true and correct knowledge of God?
C. When he is so known, that the honor, which is his due, is rendered to him.

7 M. What is the true method of rendering him due honor?
C. It is to put our whole trust in him; to serve him by obedience to his will, all our life; to call upon him in all our necessities, seeking in him salvation, and every good thing which can be desired; and finally, to acknowledge, both in the heart and with the mouth, that he is the sole author of all blessings.

8 M. But that we may discuss these things in order, and explain them more fully, which is the first head of your division?
C. That we should place our whole confidence in God.

9 M. How is that to be done?
C. By acknowledging him, Almighty and perfectly good.

10 M. Is this sufficient?
C. By no means.

11 M. Why not?
C. Because we do not deserve that he should exert his power for our assistance, or manifest his goodness for our benefit.

12 M. What more is needful?
C. That each one of us be fully convinced that God loves him, and that he is willing to be to him a Father and a Savior.

13 M. But how will that be evident to us?

C. Truly from his word, in which he declares to us his mercy, and testifies his love for us, in Christ.

14 M. The foundation and beginning of confidence in God is then, the knowledge of him in Christ?

C. Entirely.

15 M. Now I would hear from you, in a few words, the sum of this knowledge?

C. It is contained in the Confession of Faith, or rather Formula of Confession, which all Christians have always held in general among themselves. It is commonly called the Symbol of the Apostles, which has been received from the beginning of the Church among all the pious; and which was either taken from the mouth of the Apostles, or faithfully collected from their writings.

16 M. Repeat it.

C. I believe in God the Father Almighty, Maker of Heaven and earth; and in Jesus Christ, his only Son, our Lord, who was conceived by the Holy Ghost, born of the virgin Mary, suffered under Pontius Pilate was crucified, dead, and buried. He descended into Hell. The third day he arose from the dead. He ascended into Heaven, and sits at the right hand of God the Father Almighty; from thence he shall come to judge the living and the dead. I believe in the Holy Ghost, the Holy Catholic Church, the communion of Saints, the forgiveness of sins, the resurrection of the body, and the life everlasting, Amen.

17 M. That each head may be understood, into how many parts shall we divide this Confession?

JOHN CALVIN'S 1554 GENEVA CATECHISM

C. Into four principal ones.

18 M. What are they?
C. The first respects God, the Father, the second, Jesus Christ, his Son, which embraces also the whole subject of man's redemption, the third, the Holy Spirit, and the fourth, the Church, and the benefits of God towards it.

19 M. Since there is but one God, why do you name three; the Father, the Son, and the Holy Spirit?
C. Because, in the one substance of God, we must consider the Father, as the beginning and origin or first cause of all things, then the Son, who is his eternal wisdom, and lastly the Holy Spirit, as the power of God, spread abroad through all things, which yet perpetually dwells in him.

20 M. You mean then, that there is no absurdity, although we determine that these three distinct persons are in the one God-head and that God is not therefore divided.
C. It is so.

21 M. Recite the first part of the Creed.
C. I believe in God the Father Almighty, Maker of Heaven and Earth.

22 M. Why do you call him, Father?
C. Chiefly as it respects Jesus Christ, who is the eternal word of God begotten of him from eternity, and sent into this world and declared to be his Son. From hence also we understand, that since God is the Father of Jesus Christ, he is a Father to us also.

23 M. In what sense do you give him the name of Almighty?

C. Not in this manner, that he should have power and not exercise it. But that he holds all things under his hand and management, to govern the world by his Providence, to order it after his own will, and to command all creatures as it pleases him.

24 M. You do not then imagine an idle power of God, but you consider him to be one, who has always a hand prepared for operation, so that nothing is done but by him and his appointment.
C. It is so.

25. M. Why do you add, Maker or Creator of Heaven and Earth?
C. In as much as he has made himself known to us by his works; in which also he is to be sought by us (Romans 1:20). For our understandings are not capable of comprehending his essence. The world itself, therefore, is as it were a glass, in which we may discern him as far as it is for our benefit to know him.

26 M. By heaven and earth, do you not understand the whole creation?
C. Yes, truly. These two words include all things that exist in heaven and in earth.

27 M. But why do you call God Creator only, since it is much more excellent to guard and preserve the Creation in its order, than to have once created?
C. It is not indeed so much as intimated, by this expression, that God at once created his works, so that he might cast off the care of them afterwards. But it is rather to be accounted, that as he framed the world in the beginning, so he still

preserves it, and that the earth and all other things abide, only as they are preserved by his power and management. Besides, as he upholds all things by his hand, it is evident that he is the supreme Moderator and Lord of all. Since then he is the Creator of heaven and earth, it becomes us to understand him to be the One, who by his wisdom, power, and goodness, governs the whole course and order of nature, who is alike the author of the rain and the drought, of the hail and other tempests, and of fair weather, who makes the earth fruitful by his bounty, and by withdrawing his hand, again renders it barren; from when alike come health and disease, to whose dominion, all things are subject, and to whose will, all things are obedient.

28 M. What then shall I think of devils and wicked men? Shall I say that these also are in subjection to him?
C. Although God does not influence them by his Spirit; yet he restrains them by his power, as with a bridle, that they cannot move themselves, except as he permits. — Moreover, he makes them the servants of his will, so that they are constrained to pursue, unwillingly and without their intention, his pleasure.

29 M. What benefit do you derive from the knowledge of this subject?
C. Very great benefit. For it would go ill with us, if anything was permitted to devils and wicked men, without the will of God. In that case, knowing ourselves exposed to their perverseness, the tranquility of our minds would be destroyed. But now we rest in safety, believing them to be curbed by the will of God, and held in by restraint, so that they can do nothing but by his permission and especially

since God presents himself to us as our guardian and defender.

30 M. Now let us proceed to the second part of the Creed.
C. That is — And in Jesus Christ his only Son, our Lord, who was conceived by the Holy Ghost, born of the virgin Mary, suffered under Pontius Pilate was crucified, dead, and buried. He descended into Hell.

31 M. What is summarily contained in this?
C. That the Son of God is our Savior; and at the same time it explains the manner in which he has redeemed us from death, and obtained life for us.

32 M. What is the meaning of the name, Jesus, by which you call him.
C. That name in Greek signifies Savior. The Latins have no proper name, by which its force can be well expressed. Therefore the word Savior was commonly received. Besides, the Angel gave this appellation to the Son of God by the command of God himself (Matthew 1:21).

33 M. Is this of more weight, than if men had given it to him?
C. Altogether. For since God would have him so called he must of necessity be truly what he is called.

34 M. What then does the word, Christ, signify?
C. By this title, his office is still better expressed. For it signifies, that he was anointed, for a Prophet, Priest, and King.

35 M. How do you know that?

C. Because the Scriptures apply anointing to these three uses, and also often ascribe to Christ, these three offices, which we mentioned.

36 M. With what kind of oil was he anointed?
C. Not with visible—not with such as was used in the consecration of ancient Kings, Priests, and Prophets—but with more excellent oil. That is by the grace of the Holy Spirit, which is the substance represented by that external anointing.

37 M. What is the nature of that kingdom of his, of which you speak?
C. It is spiritual, as it is governed by the word and Spirit of God, which bring with them righteousness and life.

38 M. What is the nature of his Priesthood?
C. It is the office and prerogative of standing in the presence of God, for obtaining his favor, and for appeasing his wrath, by the oblation of a sacrifice, which is acceptable to him.

39 M. In what sense, do you call Christ a Prophet?
C. Because when he came into the world, he declared himself the Ambassador of the Father, and the Interpreter of his will among men. And for this purpose, that having fully explained the will of the Father, he might put an end to all revelations and prophecies.

40 M. But do you receive any benefit from this?
C. Truly all these things have no other object, but our good. For Christ was endowed with those things of the Father that he might impart them to us, and that we all might partake of his fullness.

41 M. Explain this to me a little more fully.
C. He was filled with the Holy Spirit, and enriched with all the fullness of its gifts, that he might impart them to us, and to each one, according to the measure, which the Father knew to be expedient for us. Thus from him, as the one and only fountain, we draw whatever we have of spiritual good

42 M. What does his kingly office profit us?
C. By it we are enabled to live pious and holy lives in liberty of conscience, are endowed with his spiritual riches, and also armed with that power which enables us to overcome the flesh, the world, sin, and the devil, those perpetual enemies of our souls.

43 M. What purpose does the Priesthood of Christ answer?
C. Chiefly as by this means, he is our Mediator, who reconciles us to the Father. And also that a way is opened for us to the Father, that we may come into his presence with confidence, and offer ourselves and all that is ours to him for a sacrifice. And hence, you may understand in what manner he makes us his, by his Priesthood.

44 M. The prophetic office still remains?
C. As the office of master was bestowed upon the Son of God for his people, the end is that he might illuminate them in the true knowledge of the Father, instruct them in the truth, and make them the family-disciples of God.

45 M. This then is the conclusion of all you have said. The name, Christ, comprehends three offices, which the Father conferred on the Son, that he might abundantly communicate their power and fruit unto his own.

C. It is so.

46 M. Why do you call him the only Son of God, since God distinguishes us all, by that appellation?
C. Because, if we are the sons of God, we have it not from nature. Only by grace and adoption does God hold us in that condition. But the Lord Jesus, who is begotten of the substance of the Father, and is of the same essence with him, is by the best right called the only Son of God since he alone is so, by nature (John 1:1; Ephesians 1:3; Hebrews 1:1).

47 M. You understand, then, that this honor is due to him by the right of nature, and is personally his own. It is communicated to us by gratuitous kindness, in as much as we are his members.
C. Entirely. Therefore in respect to this communication, he is called the first born among many brethren (Romans 8:29; Colossians 1:15, 18).

48 M. In what sense do you understand him to be our Lord?
C. As he is appointed by the Father, that he might have us under his dominion, that he should administer the kingdom of God in heaven and on earth, and should be the head of angels, and of believers.

49 M. What is meant by that which follows?
C. It shows the manner in which the Son is anointed by the Father, that he should be our Savior, namely, that having taken our flesh, he performed all those things which were necessary for our salvation, as they have been here declared.

50 M. What do you mean by the two sentences conceived of the Holy Ghost and born of the Virgin Mary?
C. That he was formed by the miraculous and secret power of the Holy Spirit, in the womb of the Virgin, of her substance, that he should be the true seed of David, as was foretold by the Prophets (Psalm 132:11; Matthew 1:1; Luke 1:32).

51 M. Was it then needful that he should put on our flesh?
C. Certainly, because it was necessary that man's disobedience to God should be expiated also in human nature. Nor indeed otherwise would he have been our Mediator, to accomplish the reconciliation of men with God (Romans 3:25; 1 Timothy 2:5; Hebrews 4:15; 5:7).

52 M. You say then that it behooved Christ to be made man, so that, as in our person, he might fulfill the office of our Savior.
C. So I think, for it is necessary for us to recover in him, whatever is wanting in ourselves, which cannot otherwise be done.

53 M. But why was his generation effected by the Holy Spirit, and not rather in the common and unusual manner?
C. In as much as the seed of man is wholly corrupted, it became the office of the Holy Spirit to interpose in the generation of the Son of God, lest he should he affected by that contagion, and that he might be endowed with the most perfect purity.

54 M. Hence then we learn, that he who is to sanctify others should be free from every blemish, endowed from the

womb with original purity, entirely consecrated to God, and undefiled with any corruption of the human race.

C. So I understand it.

55 M. Why do you pass immediately from his birth to his death, omitting the whole history of his life?

C. Because the Creed here treats only of those points which are the chief things of our redemption, and which contain in them as it were, its substance.

56 M. Why then do you add the name of Pontius Pilate, under whom he suffered, and not say, in one word, that he was dead?

C. That not only respects the truth of the history, but proves also, that his death was inflicted by a judicial sentence.

57 M. Explain this more fully.

C. He died that he might bear the punishment due to us, and in this manner deliver us from it. But as we all, as we were sinners, were exposed to the judgment of God, that he might suffer it in our stead, he was pleased to place himself before an earthly judge, and to be condemned by his mouth, so that we might be absolved before the throne of the heavenly Judge.

58 M. But Pilate pronounced him innocent, therefore he was not condemned as a malefactor (Matthew 27:24).

C. It becomes us to observe both these points. For thus the judge gives the testimony of his innocence, that it might be witnessed, that he suffered not for his own sins, but for ours. Yet, at the same time, he was condemned, in solemn form, by the same sentence, that it might be manifest, that by undergoing, as our substitute, the punishment which we merited, he might deliver us from it.

59 M. It is well said. For if he had been a sinner, he would not have been a fit surety for suffering the punishment of the sins of others. Yet that his condemnation might be accounted to us for absolution, it became him to be numbered among malefactors.
C. So I understand it.

60 M. As to his being crucified, has this anything of more moment, than if he had suffered any other kind of death?
C. Yes, as the Apostle informs, when he says, that he was hanged on a tree, that by bearing our curse in himself, we might be delivered from it. For that kind of death was accursed of God (Galatians 3:13; Deuteronomy 21:23).

61 M. What? Is not reproach fixed on the Son of God, when he is said to be subjected to a curse, even in the sight of God?
C. By no means. For by receiving it, he abolished it. Nor did he cease, at that time, to be blessed, when he enriched us with his benefits.

62 M. Proceed.
C. Since death was a punishment laid upon man, on account of sin, the Son of God endured it, and by enduring conquered it. And that it might be more fully manifested, that he endured a real death, he would be placed in a tomb, like other men.

63 M. But it does not appear that we derive any advantage from this victory, since we all die.

C. That is no objection. Death is nothing now to believers, but a passage to a better life.

64 M. Hence it follows, that death is no more to be dreaded as a formidable thing. But we must follow Christ our Leader with an intrepid mind, who, as he did not himself perish in death, will not suffer us to perish.
C. So we must do.

65 M. What is to be understood, as to what is immediately added concerning his descent into hell (Acts 2:24)?
C. That he not only suffered a natural death, which is the separation of soul and body, but also the pains of death; as Peter calls them. And by this phrase I understand those dreadful agonies, by which his soul was distressed.

66 M. Relate to me the cause and manner of this suffering.
C. As he placed himself before the tribunal of God, that he might make satisfaction for sinners, it became him to be tortured with horrible distress of soul, as if he was forsaken of God — nay as if he was hated of God. He was in these pains, when he cried to his "Father, My God, my God, why hast thou forsaken me!"

67 M. Was the Father then displeased with him?
C. By no means. But he exercised this severity towards him, that it might be fulfilled which was spoken by Isaiah the Prophet — "He was wounded for our transgressions, he was bruised for our iniquities" (Isaiah 53:4-5).

68 M. Since he is God, how could he be seized with this kind of horror, as if he was forsaken of God?

C. We must consider that he was reduced to this necessity, according to the affections of his human nature. And that this might be done, his Divinity in the meantime retired, that is, did not exert its power.

69 M. But how, again, can it be, that Christ, who is the Savior of the world, should be subjected to this condemnation?
C. He did not so submit to it as to remain under it. For he was not so seized by those horrors, which have been mentioned as to be overcome by them, but rather struggling with the power of hell, he subdued and destroyed it.

70 M. Hence we learn the difference between the torment of conscience, which he sustained, and that by which sinners are tortured, who are pursued by the hand of an offended God. For what in him was temporary, in them is eternal, and what in him was only the piercing of a needle's point, is in them a deadly sword wounding to the heart.
C. So it is. For the Son of God, in the midst of these pains, did not cease to hope in the Father; but sinners, condemned by the judgment of God, rush into desperation, rage against him, and press on even to open blasphemies.

71 M. Are we able to learn from hence, what fruit believers derive from the death of Christ?
C. Yes. First, we perceive him to be a sacrifice, by which he expiated our sins before God. Thus, the wrath of God being appeased, he brought us back into favor with him. Secondly, that his blood is a fountain, in which our souls are purged from all pollution. Lastly, that by his death our sins are so blotted out, that they shall not come into remembrance before God, and thus the hand writing, which held us as guilty, is erased and abolished.

72 M. Does the death of Christ bring no other benefit to us?
C. Yes, it truly does. For by its efficacy (if indeed we are the true members of Christ) our old man is crucified, the body of sin is so destroyed, that the depraved lusts of the flesh reign no more in us.

73 M. Proceed to other things in the second part.
C. It follows — The third day he arose again from the dead. By which he proved himself, the conqueror of sin and death. — For by his resurrection, he swallowed up death, broke the bonds of Satan, and reduced his whole power to nothing.

74 M. How manifold are the benefits which we derive from his resurrection?
C. Three fold. First, by it, righteousness is obtained for us. Second, it is a sure pledge of our resurrection to a glorious immortality. And third, by its power, we are even now raised to newness of life, that we may live in pure and holy obedience to the will of God (Romans 4:25; 1 Corinthians 15:22; Romans 6:4).

75 M. Let us attend to the next point.
C. He ascended into Heaven.

76 M. Did he so ascend into heaven, that he is no more on earth?
C. Yes, truly. For after he had finished all those things, commanded him of his Father, and which were requisite for our salvation, there was no occasion why he should be longer conversant on earth.

77 M. What benefit do we derive from this ascension?
C. The fruit is twofold. For in as much as Christ has entered into heaven in our name, as he descended to the earth for our sakes, he has opened to us also that door, which, on account of sin, was before shut. Secondly, he appears in the presence of God, as our Intercessor and Advocate.

78 M. But has he, by ascending to heaven, so departed, as to be no more with us?
C. By no means. For he promised, that he would be with us even to the end of the world.

79 M. But by his dwelling with us, are we to understand his bodily presence?
C. No. For the manner in which his body is received into heaven, is one thing. The presence of his power, which is diffused everywhere, is another.

80 M. In what sense do you say that he sits at the right hand of God the Father?
C. These words signify, that the Father has given to him the dominion of heaven and earth, that he should govern all things (Matthew 27:20).

81 M. What do you understand by this right hand and by this sitting?
C. It is a similitude taken from earthly Princes, who are accustomed to place, at their right hand, those who act as their ministers.

82 M. Do you mean the same thing, as that which Paul declares that Christ is constituted head over all things to the Church, and being exalted above all principalities, he hath

obtained a name which is above every name (Ephesians 1:22; Philippians 2:9).
C. Yes, it is so.

83 M. Let us pass to that which follows.
C. From thence he shall come to judge the quick and the dead — The meaning of which words is, that he will as openly come from heaven, to judge the world, as he was seen to ascend into heaven (Acts 1:11).

84 M. As the day of judgment will not be till the end of the world, how do you say that there will be some of mankind remaining as it is appointed unto all men once to die (Hebrews 9:37).
C. Paul answers this question, when he says that those who are then alive shall be made new by a sudden change, that the corruption of the flesh being put off, they may put on incorruption (1 Corinthians 15:5; 1 Thessalonians 4:7).

85 M. You understand then that this change will be the same to them? Like death it will be the abolishing of the first nature and the beginning of a new life?
C. So I understand it.

86 M. May not our minds receive consolation from this that Christ is one day to be the Judge of the world?
C. Yes, singular consolation. For by this we certainly know that he will come, for our salvation.

87 M. We should not then so fear this judgment, as to have it fill us with dread.

C. By no means. For we shall then stand before the tribunal of the Judge, who is also our Advocate; and who will receive us into his confidence and charge.

88 M. Let us now come to the third part.
C. That is concerning Faith in the Holy Spirit.

89 M. Of what use is that to us?
C. Truly in this respect, that we may know, that as God has redeemed and saved us by his Son, so he will make us partakers of this redemption and salvation by the Holy Spirit.

90 M. In what manner?
C. In as much as we have cleansing by the blood of Christ; so it is necessary, that our consciences be sprinkled with it, that they may be purified (1 Peter 1:2; 1 John 1:7).

91 M. This requires a clearer exposition.
C. I understand, that the Holy Spirit, dwelling in our hearts, operates so that we may experience the power of Christ. For it is by the illumination of the Holy Spirit that we understand the benefits we derive from Christ, by his persuasion they are sealed in our hearts, and he prepares in us a place for them. He also regenerates us and makes us new creatures. Therefore, whatever gifts are offered us in Christ, we receive by the power of the Spirit (Romans 8:11; Ephesians 1:13).

92 M. Let us proceed.
C. The fourth part follows in which we profess to believe in the Holy Catholic Church.

93 M. What is the Church?
C. The body and society of believers, whom God has predestinated unto eternal life.

94 M. Is this article necessary to be believed?
C. Yes, truly, unless we would render the death of Christ without effect, and account all that we have said, for nothing. For this is the sole purpose of all, that there should be a Church.

95 M. You understand then, that the cause of salvation has been hitherto treated of, and its foundation shown, when you explained, that we were received into the favor of God, by the merits and intercession of Christ, and that this grace is confirmed in us by the power of the Holy Spirit. But now the effect of all these is to be unfolded, so that from the very subject itself, Faith may be more firmly established.
C. It is so.

96 M. But why do you call the Church Holy?
C. Because those whom God elects, he justifies, and purifies in holiness and innocence of life, to make his glory shine forth in them. And this is what Paul means, when he says, that Christ sanctified the Church, which he redeemed, that it might be glorious and pure from every spot (Romans 8:30; Ephesians 5:25).

97 M. What do you mean by the epithet Catholic or universal?
C. By that we are taught, that as there is one head of all believers, so it becomes all to be united in one body, that there may be one Church and no more, spread throughout all the world (Ephesians 4:15; 1 Corinthians 12:12).

98 M. What is the meaning of what is next added, the communion of saints?

C. This is laid down, to express more clearly the unity which is among the members of the Church. At the same time, it intimates, that whatever benefits God bestows on the Church, respect the common good of all, as all have a communion among themselves.

99 M. But is this holiness, which you attribute to the Church, already perfect?

C. Not yet, not so long, indeed, as it is militant in this world. For it will always labor under infirmities. Nor will it ever be entirely purified from the remains of corruption, until it shall be completely united to Christ its head, by whom it is sanctified.

100 M. Can this Church be otherwise known, than as it is discerned by Faith?

C. There is indeed a visible Church of God, which he has designated to us by certain signs and tokens. But we now treat expressly of the congregation of those, whom he has elected to salvation. But this is neither known by signs, nor at any time discerned by the eyes.

101 M. What article follows next?

C. I believe the forgiveness of sins.

102 M. What does the word forgiveness signify?

C. That God, by his gratuitous goodness, will pardon and remit the sins of believers, so that they shall neither come into judgment, nor have punishment exacted of them.

103 M. Hence it follows, that we can by no means merit, by personal satisfactions, that pardon of sins, which we obtain from the Lord.

C. It is true. For Christ alone, by suffering the penalty, has finished the satisfaction. As to ourselves, we have nothing at all, which we can offer to God as a compensation. We receive the benefit of pardon from his pure goodness and liberality.

104 M. Why do you connect forgiveness of sins with the Church?

C. Because no one obtains it, only as he is first united to the people of God, and perseveringly cherishes this union with the body of Christ even to the end; and in that manner gives evidence, that he is a true member of the Church.

105 M. By this rule you determine, that there is no condemnation or destruction, except to those who are without the Church?

C. It is so. For from those who make a separation from the body of Christ, and by factions destroy its unity, all hope of salvation is cut off, in so far as they continue in this separation.

106 M. Recite the last article.

C. I believe the resurrection of the body and the life everlasting.

107 M. For what purpose is this article of Faith put in the Confession?

C. To admonish us that our happiness is not to be placed in this world. The knowledge of this has a twofold advantage and use. By it we are taught, first, that this world is to be passed through by us, merely as strangers — that we may think continually of our departure, and not suffer our hearts to be entangled with earthly anxieties. And secondly, that we should not, in the meantime, despair in our minds, but patiently wait for those things which are as yet hidden and concealed from our eyes, being the fruits of grace, laid up for us in Christ, until the day of revelation.

108 M. What will be the order of this resurrection?
C. Those who were before dead will receive the same bodies in which they dwelt on earth, but endowed with a new quality, that is, to be no more annoyed by death and corruption. But those who shall be living at that day, God will marvelously raise up with a sudden change (1 Corinthians 15:53).

109 M. But will it be common at once to the just and the unjust?
C. There will be one resurrection of all. But the condition will be different. Some will be raised to salvation and glory. Others will be raised to condemnation, and final misery (Matthew 25:46; John 5:29).

110 M. Why then is eternal life spoken, of, in the Creed and no mention made of the wicked?
C. Because nothing is treated of in that summary but what relates to the consolation of pious minds. Therefore, those blessings only are considered which the Lord has prepared for his servants. For this reason nothing is said about the condition which awaits the wicked, whom we know to be aliens from the kingdom of God.

111 M. Since we hold the foundation on which Faith depends, it will be easy to infer from thence the definition of true Faith.
C. It is so, and thus we may define it — Faith is the certain and stable knowledge of the paternal benevolence of God towards us, according to his testimony in the Gospel, that he will be to us, for the sake of Christ, a Father and a Savior.

112 M. Do we obtain that of ourselves, or do we receive it from God?
C. The scriptures teach us, that it is the special gift of God, and experience confirms the testimony.

113 M. Inform me what experience.
C. Truly, our understandings are too weak to comprehend that spiritual knowledge of God, which is revealed to us by Faith. Our hearts have too strong a propensity to distrust God, and to put a perverse confidence in ourselves or the creatures, for us to submit to him of our own mere motion. But the Holy Spirit makes us capable, by his own illumination, of understanding those things, which would otherwise very far exceed our capacity, and forms in us a sure persuasion, by sealing in our hearts the promises of salvation.

114 M. What benefit arises to us from this Faith, when we have once obtained it?
C. It justifies us before God, and by this justification makes us heirs of eternal life.

115 M. What? Are not men justified by good works, when by living an innocent and holy life, they study to approve themselves to God?

C. If anyone could be found thus perfect, he might well be called just. But since we are all sinners, in many ways guilty before God, that worthiness which may reconcile us to him must be sought by us in some other way.

116 M. But are all the works of men so polluted, and of no value, that they deserve no favor with God?
C. In the first place, all those things which proceed from us, as they are properly called ours, are polluted, and therefore avail nothing, but to displease God, and be rejected by him.

117 M. You say then, that before we are born again, and created anew by the Spirit of God, we can do nothing but sin as a corrupt tree brings forth only corrupt fruit (Matthew 7:18).
C. It is wholly so. For whatever appearance our works may have in the eyes of men, they are altogether evil, as long as the heart is corrupt at which God especially looks.

118 M. Hence you infer, that we cannot, by any merits of our own, come before God and challenge his favor. Rather, in all our undertakings and pursuits, we expose ourselves to his wrath and condemnation.
C. So I think. Therefore it is of his mere mercy, and not from any respect to our works, that he freely embraces us in Christ, and holds us accepted, by accounting that righteousness of his, which is accepted by us, as our own and not imputing our sins unto us (Titus 3:5).

119 M. In what manner then do you say that we are justified by Faith?

C. When by a sure confidence of heart, we embrace the promises of the gospel, then we obtain possession of this righteousness.

120 M. You mean this then that this righteousness is so to be received by Faith as it is offered unto us, of God, in the gospel.
C. Yes.

121 M. But when God has once embraced us, are not those works acceptable to him, which we do by the influence of the Holy Spirit?
C. They please him so far as he freely renders them worthy by his own favor, but not from the merit of their own worthiness.

122 M. But since they proceed from the Holy Spirit, do they not merit his acceptance?
C. No, because they have always some mixture of pollution from the infirmity of the flesh, by which they are defiled.

123 M. Whence then, and in what way, do they become pleasing to God?
C. It is Faith alone which renders them acceptable. Then we may rest assuredly on this confidence, that they shall not come to the sentence of the last trial, as God will not examine them by the rule of his severity. But covering their impurities and spots, by the purity of Christ, he will account them as if they were perfect.

124 M. Shall we understand from thence, that a Christian is justified by his works, after he is called of God, or that he

can obtain by their merit, that he should be loved of God, whose love to us is eternal life?

C. By no means. Let us rather believe what is written, that no man living can be justified before God; and therefore we pray, "Enter not into judgment with us" (Psalm 143:2).

125 M. Must we then conclude, that the good works of believers are useless?

C. No, for God has promised a reward to them, both in this world and in the life to come. But this reward proceeds from the gratuitous love of God as from a fountain as he first embraces us as sons. Then by blotting out the remembrance of our sins, he follows with his favor those things which we do.

126 M. But can that righteousness be separated from good works so that he who has that may be destitute of these?

C. This cannot be done. For to believe in Christ is to receive him as he offers himself to us. Now he not only promises to us deliverance from death, and reconciliation with God, but at the same time also, the grace of the Holy Spirit, by which we are regenerated in newness of life. It is necessary that these things be united together, unless we would divide Christ from himself,

127 M. It follows from this, that Faith is the root, from which all good works originate and cannot, by any means, make us slothful about them.

C. It is true. And therefore the whole doctrine of the gospel is contained in these two points, Faith and Repentance.

128 M. What is Repentance?

C. It is a hatred of sin and a love of righteousness, proceeding from the fear of God leading us to a denial and mortification of the flesh, so that we may give up ourselves to be governed by the Holy Spirit, and perform all the actions of our lives in obedience to the will of God.

129 M. But this last point was, in the division, laid down in the beginning, when you stated the true method of honoring God.
C. Yes, it was then observed, that the true and legitimate rule of glorifying God, was to obey his will.

130 M. How so?
C. Because the service which God approves is not that which we may please to feign to ourselves, but that which he has prescribed by his own counsel.

II. OF THE LAW. THAT IS, OF THE TEN COMMANDMENTS OF GOD

131 M. What rule of life has God given to us?
C. His Law.

132 M. What does that contain?
C. It is divided into two parts. The first contains four commandments, and the other six. Thus the whole law is summed up in ten commandments.

133 M. Who is the author of this division?
C. God himself, who delivered it to Moses written on two tables; and it is often declared to be comprised in ten commandments (Exodus 24:12; 32:15; 34:1; Deuteronomy 4:13; 10:4).

134 M. What is the subject of the first table?
C. It treats of the duties of religion towards God.

135 M. What is the subject of the second table?
C. Our duties to men, and our conduct towards them.

136 M. Which is the first commandment?
C. Hear, Israel, I am the Lord thy God which have brought thee out of the land of Egypt, out of the house of bondage. Thou shall have no other gods before me (Exodus 20:2; Deuteronomy 5:6).

137 M. Explain these words.
C. The first part is used as a preface to the whole law. For in calling himself the Lord or Jehovah, he establishes his right and authority to command. Next, by declaring himself bur God, he would render his law acceptable to us. Lastly, these words also imply, that he is our Savior and as he distinguishes us by this privilege, it is just on our part that we present ourselves to him as his willing people.

138 M. But does not the deliverance from the bondage of Egypt respect peculiarly the people of Israel?
C. I confess it does, as to the work itself, but there is another kind of deliverance, which pertains equally to all men — For he has delivered us all from the spiritual servitude of sin and the tyranny of the devil.

139 M. Why does he remind us of that in the preface to his law?

C. To admonish us that we shall be guilty of the highest ingratitude, unless we entirely devote ourselves in obedience to him.

140 M. What is required in the first commandment?
C. That we should render to him the honor, in full, which is his due; without giving any part of it to another.

141 M. What is the peculiar honor, which must not be transferred to another?
C. To worship him, to place our whole trust in him, to pray to him, and, in a word, to ascribe to him all those things which belong to his Majesty,

142 M. What are we taught by the words "before me?"
C. That nothing is so hidden, as to be concealed from him. He is the witness and judge of all our secret thoughts, and that he requires, not merely the honor of an external confession, but also the sincere devotion of the heart.

143 M. Which is the second commandment?
C. Thou shalt not make unto thee, any graven image, or any likeness of anything that is in heaven above, or that is in the earth beneath, or that is in the water under the earth. Thou shalt not bow down thyself to them nor serve them.

144 M. Does God wholly forbid the painting or sculpturing of any images?
C. He forbids only these two — The making of images, for the purpose of representing God, or for worshipping him.

145 M. Why is it forbidden to represent God, by a visible image?

C. Because there is nothing in him, who is an eternal and incomprehensible Spirit, that resembles a corporeal, corruptible, and inanimate figure (Deuteronomy 4:15; Acts 17:29; Romans 1:23).

146 M. You judge it then to be dishonorable to his Majesty, to attempt to represent him thus.
C. Yes.

147 M. What sort of worship is forbidden, by this commandment?
C. That we should address ourselves in prayer to a statue or image, prostrate ourselves before it. Or by kneeling, or any other signs, give honor to it, as though God therein would present himself to us.

148 M. It is not then to be understood that the commandment condemns painting and sculpturing; but only, that images are forbidden to be made for the purpose of seeking or worshipping God in them or, what is the same thing, that we should worship them in honor of God, or by any means abuse them to superstition and idolatry.
C. It is so.

149 M. What is required in this commandment?
C. As in the first, God declared that he was alone to be adored and worshipped. So in this, he shows us the true form of worship, by which he would recall us from all superstition, and other depraved and corrupt forgeries.

150 M. Let us proceed.
C. He adds a sanction, "I am the Lord thy God almighty and jealous, visiting the iniquity of the Fathers upon the

Children unto the third and fourth generation of them that hate me."

151 M. Why does he mention his power or might?
C. To show us, that he is able to vindicate his glory.

152 M. What does he indicate by the word jealous?
C. That he can endure no equal or partner. That having given himself to us by his own infinite goodness, so he will have us to be wholly his own. And it is the chastity of our souls, to be dedicated to him, and to cleave wholly to him. As on the other hand, they are said to be defiled with adultery, when they turn away from him, to superstition.

153 M. In what sense is it said "visiting the iniquity of the Fathers upon the Children?"
C. That he may awaken in us greater terror, he not only threatens that he will take punishment of those who transgress but that their offspring also shall be under a curse.

154 M. But is it consistent with the equity of God, to punish one for the fault of another?
C. If we consider the true state of mankind, the question will be solved. For by nature, we are all exposed to the curse. Nor is there any reason that we should complain of God, when he leaves us in this condition. But as he proves his love towards the pious, by blessing their posterity, so he executes his vengeance upon the wicked, by withholding his blessing from their children.

155 M. Proceed to the rest.

C. That he may allure us by his kindness, he promises, that he will show mercy, towards all, who love him and keep his commandments, to a thousand generations.

156 M. Does this intimate that the obedience of a godly man shall be for the salvation of all his children, however wicked?
C. By no means. But in this manner, he would exhibit himself as extending his bounty, thus far, towards believers, that out of favor to them, he would show kindness to their offspring not only by prospering their worldly affairs but also by sanctifying their souls, that they should be numbered among his flock.

157 M. But this does not appear to be continually done.
C. I confess it. For as the Lord reserves this liberty to himself, to show mercy when he pleases to the children of the wicked. So he has not so restricted his favor to the offspring of believers, but that he casts off those, whom it seems him good, according to his own will. Yet he so manages this, as to make it evident that the promise is not a vain and fallacious thing (Romans 11).

158 M. Why does he mention a thousand generations, in showing mercy, and only three or four, in executing punishment?
C. That he may show himself more inclined to kindness and mercy, than he is to severity. As in another place, he testifies — That he is ready to forgive, but slow to anger (Exodus 34:6; Psalms 103:8; 145:8).

159 M. Which is the third commandment?
C. Thou shalt not take the, name of the Lord thy God in vain.

160 M. What is forbidden in this commandment?
C. It forbids us, to abuse the name of God, not only by perjury but by all unnecessary oaths.

161 M. May the name of God be at all lawfully used in oaths?
C. Yes truly, when introduced on a just occasion. First, in establishing the truth. Secondly, in matters of importance, for preserving mutual peace and charity among men.

162 M. Is it not then the sole purpose of this commandment, to forbid those oaths, by which the name of God is profaned and dishonored?
C. This one object being proposed, it admonishes us generally never to introduce the name of God in public, unless with fear and reverence, and for his glory. For as it is holy, we must take heed, by all means, lest we should appear to treat it with contempt, or give to others the occasion of despising it.

163 M. How is this to be done?
C. If we think or speak of God or his works, we must do it, in a manner that will honor him.

164 M. What follows?
C. The threatening — For the Lord will not hold him guiltless, who takes his name in vain.

165 M. Since God, in other places, declares that he will punish the transgressors of his law, what more is contained in this?

C. By this he would declare, how highly he estimates the glory of his name. We may be the more careful to hold it in reverence when we see him prepared to take vengeance on any one, who profanes it.

166 M. Let us proceed to the fourth commandment.
C. Remember the Sabbath day to keep it holy. Six days shalt thou labor, and do all thy work; but the seventh day is the Sabbath of the Lord thy God. On it thou shalt not do any work, thou, nor thy son, nor thy daughter, thy man servant nor thy maid servant, nor thy cattle nor the stranger, that is within thy gates. For in six days the Lord made heaven and earth, the sea and all that in them is, and rested the seventh day. Therefore the Lord blessed the Sabbath day and hallowed it.

167 M. Does he command us to labor the six days that we may rest the seventh?
C. Not simply. Permitting six days to the labors of men, he excepts the seventh, that it may be devoted to rest.

168 M. But does he forbid us any labor on that day?
C. This commandment has a distinct and peculiar reason. In so far as the observation of rest was a part of the ceremonial law it was abrogated at the coming of Christ.

169 M. Do you say that this commandment respected the Jews only, and was therefore merely temporary?
C. Yes, so far as it was ceremonial.

170 M. What then? Is there anything in it besides what is ceremonial?
C. Yes; it was given for three reasons.

171 M. State them to me.

C. To prefigure a spiritual rest. To preserve the polity of the Church. And for the relief of servants.

172 M. What do you understand by a spiritual rest?

C. When we rest from our own works, that God may perform his work in us.

173 M. How is that done?

C. When we crucify our flesh that is, renounce our own understanding, that we may be governed by the Spirit of God.

174 M. Is it sufficient that this be done on the seventh day merely?

C. No, it must be done continually. For when we have once begun, we must proceed through the whole course of our life.

175 M. Why then is a particular day appointed to represent this rest?

C. It is not at all necessary that the figure should, in every point, agree with the substance. It is enough, if there is a resemblance according to the order of types.

176 M. Why is the seventh day appointed, rather than any other?

C. This number in scripture designates perfection. Therefore it is proper to determine its perpetuity. At the same time, it indicates that this spiritual rest can only be begun in this life; and that it will not be perfected until we depart from this world.

177 M. What does this mean that the Lord exhorts us to rest as he himself rested?

C. When God had made an end of creating the world, in six days, he devoted the seventh to the contemplation of his works. And he proposes his own example, that he may excite us more diligently to the same work. For nothing is more earnestly to be sought, than that we may be conformed to his image.

178 M. Ought this meditation of the works of God to be continual, or is it enough to appoint one of the seven days, for that purpose?

C. It is our duty to be daily exercised in that work; but on account of our weakness, one day is especially appointed, and this is the ecclesiastical polity which I mentioned.

179 M. What is the order to be observed on that day?

C. That the people assemble to hear the doctrine of Christ, to unite in the public prayers, and to offer the confession of their Faith.

180 M. Now explain the point, that the Lord in this commandment had respect also to the relief of servants.

C. It requires that some relaxation be given to those who are under the authority of others. And besides, this also tends to preserve the civil government. For where one day is devoted to rest, each one becomes accustomed to pursue his labors more orderly the rest of the time.

181 M. Now let us see how far this commandment respects us?

C. As to the ceremonial part it was abolished, when its substance was manifested in Christ.

182 M. How?
C. For example, as our old man is crucified by the power of his death, and we are raised by his resurrection to newness of life (Colossians 2:17; Romans 6:6).

183 M. What then of this commandment remains for us?
C. That we should not neglect the holy institutions, which support the spiritual government of the Church. But especially that we frequent the sacred meetings, for hearing the word of God, for celebrating the ordinances, and for joining in the public prayers, according to their appointment.

184 M. But does this figure conduce nothing more to our advantage.
C. Yes, it truly does for it brings us back to its substance. To wit, that being engrafted into the body of Christ, and becoming his members, we must cease from trusting in our own works, and resign ourselves wholly to the government of God.

185 M. Let us pass to the second table.
C. Its beginning is — Honor thy father and thy mother.

186 M. What in this place is the meaning of the word honor?
C. That with modesty and humility, children should be submissive and obedient to their parents, and treat them with reverence. That they assist them in their necessities, and repay them their own labors. These three points comprehend the honors which is due to parents.

187 M. Proceed now.

C. A promise is annexed to the commandment — That your days may be long upon the land which the Lord thy God gives you.

188 M. What is the meaning of this?

C. That those who render due honor to their parents shall, by the blessing of God, live long.

189 M. Since this life is filled with so many cares, why does God promise its long continuance, as a blessing?

C. However great are the miseries to which life is exposed, yet it is the blessing of God to believers, even on this one account. That it is a proof of his paternal favor, while he preserves and cherishes them here.

190 M. Does it follow on the other hand, that he who is snatched away from the world, prematurely and suddenly, is accursed of God?

C. By no means. But it rather happens, sometimes, as any one is beloved of God, so much the sooner he is removed from this life.

191 M. But in doing this how does God fulfill his promise?

C. Whatever of earthly good is promised of God, it becomes us to receive it under this condition, as far as it shall conduce to our spiritual benefit, and the salvation of our souls. For the order would be very preposterous, unless the good of the soul was always preferred.

192 M. What shall we say of those who are disobedient to their parents?

C. They will not only be punished in the last judgment but in this life God will also punish their bodies, either in taking them away in the flower of their age, or by some ignominious death, or by other means.

193 M. But does not the promise speak expressly of the land of Canaan?
C. It does so far as it respects the Israelites. But the promise reaches farther, and should be extended to us. For in whatever region we dwell, as the earth is the Lord's, he assigns it to us for a possession (Psalm 24:1; 85:8; 115:16).

194 M. What is there more required in this commandment?
C. Although the words express only father and mother, yet all those are to be included, who are in authority over us when the same rule is applicable to them.

195 M. When is that?
C. It is when God raises them to a superior degree of honor. For there is no authority of parents, or princes, or any rulers, no command, no honor, but what is derived from the appointment of God because thus it pleases him to govern the world for his own glory.

196 M. Which is the sixth commandment?
C. Thou shall not kill.

197 M. Does it forbid nothing but to commit murder?
C. Yes truly. For God, in this law, not only regulates the external actions, but also the affections of the heart, and these chiefly.

198 M. You seem to imply, that there is a kind of secret murder, which God here forbids us?

C. It is so. For anger, and hatred, and any revengeful desire of injuring, are accounted murder in the sight of God.

199 M. Are we sufficiently free from it, if we pursue no one with hatred?

C. By no means. In as much as the Lord, in condemning hatred, and forbidding us anything which might be injurious to our neighbor's welfare, at the same time shows himself to demand this, that we love all men from the heart and that we give diligence to defend and preserve their lives.

200 M. Which is the seventh commandment?

C. Thou shalt not commit adultery.

201 M. What is the sum of this commandment?

C. That fornication of every kind is accursed in the sight of God, and that unless we would provoke his wrath against ourselves we must diligently abstain from it.

202 M. What else does it require?

C. That the design of the Legislator be regarded which, as we said, does not rest in the external action but rather respects the affections of the heart.

203 M. What more then does it comprehend?

C. That as both our bodies and our souls are the temples of the Holy Spirit, therefore we should preserve them both chaste and pure. And also that we should modestly abstain not only from actual crimes, but even in our hearts, words, and gestures of body. Finally, that the body be kept free from all lascivious carriage, and the soul from every lust, that no part of us be defiled by the filth of impurity (1 Corinthians 3:16; 6:19; 2 Corinthians 6:16).

204 M. Which is the eighth commandment?
C. Thou shalt not steal.

205 M. Does this only forbid those thefts which are punished by human laws or does it extend farther?
C. It embraces under the word theft every kind of defrauding and circumventing, and all those evil arts by which we are intent to possess the goods of others. By it we are forbidden, either violently to seize on the goods of our neighbors, or by cunning or deceit to lay hands on them, or to endeavor to occupy them by any unjust means whatever.

206 M. Is it enough to abstain from the evil action, or is the intention also here forbidden?
C. It is. Since God is a spiritual Legislator, he wills that not only external theft fee avoided but also all those plans and counsels which at all injure others; and especially that selfishness, which seeks to grow rich by the misfortunes of our neighbors.

207 M. What is to be done, that we may obey this commandment?
C. Diligence must be given, that each one may safely possess his own.

208 M. Which is the ninth commandment?
C. Thou shalt not bear false witness against thy neighbor.

209 M. Does this merely forbid perjury in courts, or in general, all falsehood against our neighbor?
C. Under this form of expression the whole doctrine is included. That we shall not by falsehood calumniate our neighbor or by our evil speaking and detraction destroy his reputation, or bring any damage to him in his estate.

210 M. But why is public perjury expressly forbidden?
C. That we might be struck with greater horror at this vice. And it implies that if any one become accustomed to evil speaking and backbiting, from that habit the descent to perjury is rapid.

211 M. Is it not the design of this commandment, to deter us not only from evil speaking, but also from evil suspicions, and uncandid and unjust judgments?
C. It condemns both according to the reason before given. For that which is evil to do, before men, is even wicked to will before God.

212 M. What is the sum of this commandment?
C. It forbids us to think evil of our neighbors, and to indulge any propensity to defame them. And on the other hand, God commands us to be endowed with equity and humanity, that we may be studious to think well of them as far as the truth will permit; and to preserve our estimation of them entire.

213 M. Which is the tenth commandment?
C. Thou shalt not covet thy neighbor's house, thou shalt not covet thy neighbor's wife, nor his man servant, nor his maid servant, nor his ox, nor his ass, nor any thing that is thy neighbor's.

214 M. Since, as you have said, the whole law is spiritual, and the preceding commandments are designed to restrain not only the external actions. But to correct also the affections of the mind; what more is there contained in this?
C. By the other precepts God would govern and restrain the will and affections. In this, he imposes a law upon those thoughts which carry with them some degree of covetousness, although they do not ripen into an established determination.

215 M. Do you say that all even the least of those depraved desires, which seize upon believers, and come into their minds, are sins, even though they resist rather than assent to them?
C. It is surely evident, that all corrupt thoughts, although our consent is not added, proceed from the corruption of our nature. This only I say, that by this commandment, those depraved desires are condemned, which stir up and please the heart of man, although they do not draw it to a firm and deliberate purpose.

216 M. Thus far then you understand, that not only are those evil affections in which men acquiesce and to which they become subject, forbidden. But also such strict integrity is required of us that our minds must not admit any perverse desires, by which they might be stimulated to sin.
C. It is so.

217 M. Will you now give a short summary of the whole law?

C. Yes, it shall be done, in as much as we may sum it up in two heads. The first is "thou shall love the Lord thy God with all thy heart, and with all thy mind, and with all thy strength." The second is "thou shall love thy neighbor as thyself."

218 M. What is included in loving God?
C. To love him as God. That is, that he be acknowledged at once, as our Lord, our Father, and our Savior. To the love of God, therefore, must be joined a reverence of him, obedience to his will, and that confidence which ought to be placed in him.

219 M. What do you understand by the whole heart, mind, and strength?
C. That ardor of affection, which leaves no place in us for any thoughts, desires, or endeavors, which are opposed to this love.

220 M. What is the meaning of the second heading?
C. As we are by nature so prone to love ourselves, that this affection overpowers all others, so it becomes us to regulate the love of our neighbor in ourselves by this, that it may govern us in all respects, and be the rule of all our counsels and labors.

221 M. What do you understand by the word neighbor?
C. Not only kindred and friends, and those who are bound to us by some alliance, but those also who are unknown to us, and even our enemies.

222 M. But what connection have they with us?

C. They are certainly united to us by that bond, by which God binds together the whole race of men. And this is so sacred and inviolable, that it cannot be abolished by the wickedness of anyone.

223 M. You say then, that if anyone should hate us, this love is still his due; he is still our neighbor, and is so to be accounted by us because the divine constitution stands inviolable, by which this relation between us is sanctioned.
C. It is so.

224 M. As the law declares the true manner of worshipping God, must we not live wholly according to his prescription?
C. Yes truly. But we all of us labor under such infirmity, that no one fulfills it in all respects, as he ought.

225 M. Why then does God exact of us that perfection, which is above our ability?
C. He demands nothing above that excellence to which we are in duty bound. But only let us strive to reach that course of life, which his law prescribes, and although we should be at a distance from the mark, which is from perfection, the Lord will pardon us what is wanting.

226 M. Do you speak in this manner of all men, or only of believers?
C. He who is not yet regenerated by the Spirit of God, is not indeed qualified, to perform the least point of the law. Besides if we should grant someone to be found who should observe the law in some part, yet we could not from that determine that he complied with it fully in the sight of God. For he pronounces all those accursed, who do not fulfill all

things contained in the law (Deuteronomy 27:26; Galatians 3:10).

227 M. Hence we must conclude, that as there are two sorts of men, so the office of the law is twofold.
C. Yes, for among unbelievers it effects nothing only as it precludes them from all excuse before God. And this is what Paul says, when he calls it the ministration of condemnation and death. Towards believers it has a very different use (Romans 1:32; 2 Corinthians 3:6).

228 M. What use?
C. First, while they learn from it, that it is impossible for them to obtain justification by works, they are instructed in humility, which is the true preparation for seeking salvation in Christ. Secondly, that, in as much as the law demands of them more than they can perform, it excites them to seek strength of the Lord, and at the same time admonishes them of their constant guilt, lest they should presume to be proud. Lastly, It is to them like a bridle by which they are held, in the fear of God (Romans 3:20; Galatians 2:16; 3:11; 4:5).

229 M. Although then, in this earthly pilgrimage, we cannot satisfy the law, we must not account it superfluous that it demands of us such entire perfection for it points out to us the mark at which we are to aim, the goal for which we are to contend. That each one of us may strive, with zealous assiduity, according to the measure of the grace given him, to conform his life to the highest rectitude, and to be still making continual progress.
C. So I think.

230 M. Have we not in the law a perfect rule of all righteousness?
C. We have, and God requires nothing more of us, than that we should follow it. But on the other hand, he accounts and rejects as corrupt, whatever we undertake beyond what he has prescribed. Nor does he hold any other sacrifice accepted but obedience (1 Samuel 14:22; Jeremiah 7:22).

231 M. For what purpose then are so many admonitions, commands, and exhortations, constantly given by the prophets and apostles?
C. They are merely so many expositions of the law, which lead us by the hand to its obedience, and by no means draw us from it.

232 M. But does it command nothing concerning the callings of individuals?
C. As it commands us to render to each one his due, it is easy to collect from it what those personal duties are, which each one should perform, in his station and course of life. And those numerous expositions of each precept mentioned above, are repeatedly published in the scriptures. For what God summarily includes in a few words in these two tables of the law, is more fully and extensively illustrated in other parts of his word.

III. OF PRAYER

233 M. Having discoursed sufficiently concerning submission and obedience, which are the second part of the honor due to God, let us now treat of the third.
C. We called it Invocation, in as much as we betake ourselves to God in all our necessities.

234 M. Do you suppose that he alone is to be invoked?
C. Yes, for that is what he demands as the peculiar honor of his Godhead.

235 M. If it is so, how is it lawful for us to implore the assistance of men?
C. The difference is very great in these two cases. For when we invoke God, we testify, that we look nowhere else for any blessing, and that our whole defense is placed entirely in him. However, he, at the same time, permits us to seek assistance from those to whom he has given the power to help us.

236 M. You say then, that when we invoke the true God we may betake ourselves to the help and support of men, provided we do not by any means put our trust in them, and that we must no otherwise ask their aid, but as they are endowed of God with the ability of being the ministers and dispensers of his favors, for our benefit.
C. It is so. And therefore whatever benefits we receive from them, we must consider as received from God. The fact is that he bestows all those things upon us, by their agency.

237 M. But must we not give thanks to men, as often as they perform for us any office of kindness. For that is dictated by natural justice, and the law of humanity?
C. We must thank them, and for this sole reason, that God dignifies those with this honor, that those good things, which flow from the inexhaustible fountain of his fullness, are poured upon us as streams through their hands. By this method he binds us to them, and wills that we acknowledge

the obligation. Therefore, he who does not show himself grateful to men, in this way betrays also ingratitude to God.

238 M. May we conclude from hence that it is wicked to invoke either angels, or the holy servants of the Lord who have departed this life?
C. We may. For God has not assigned those services to the saints, that they should assist us. And as to the angels, although he uses their labors for our welfare, yet he will not have us pray to them.

239 M. You say, then, that whatever does not agree with the order instituted of God contravenes his will?
C. It is so, for it is a certain sign of unbelief, not to be contented with those things which God gives to us. If then we betake ourselves to the assistance of angels or departed saints, when God calls us to himself alone, if we transfer to them our confidence, which should rest entirely on him, we fall into idolatry as we indeed impart among them, that which God challenges in full as belonging to himself alone.

240 M. Now let us treat of the nature of prayer. Is it enough in prayer to utter words, or does it require the understanding and the heart?
C. Words indeed are not always necessary. But true prayer can never be offered without the understanding and the heart.

241 M. By what argument will you prove this to me?
C. Since God is a spirit, and in other duties always demands the heart from men, so he especially does in prayer, in which they converse with him. Nor does he promise himself to be close unto any, but those who call upon him in truth.

But on the other hand he holds in abomination all those who pray in hypocrisy, and not from the heart.

242 M. All those prayers are then vain and ineffectual which are made by the mouth only (Psalm 145:18; Isaiah 29:13).
C. Not only so. But they are very displeasing to God.

243 M. What disposition does God require in prayer?
C. First, that we be sensible of our poverty and wretchedness and that a sense of these should produce grief and anxiety of mind. Secondly, that we be animated with such a vehement and devout desire to obtain the favor of God, as may enkindle in us a spirit of ardent prayer.

244 M. Is that disposition natural to men, or do they derive it from the grace of God?
C. In this the assistance of God is necessary for we are altogether stupid in both those points. And it is the Spirit of God, as Paul says, who excites in our minds those unutterable groans, and creates those desires which are required in prayer (Romans 8:25; Galatians 4:6).

245 M. Does this doctrine imply that we may sit down, and indifferently wait the motions of the Spirit, and that we have no occasion to stir up ourselves to prayer?
C. Not at all but this is its tendency. When we perceive ourselves to grow cold, sluggish, and indisposed to prayer, we should betake ourselves to God, and entreat that we may be awakened by the sharp convictions of the Holy Spirit, and thus be fitted for the duty of prayer.

246 M. You do not mean, however, that there is no use for the voice in prayer?

C. By no means. The voice is often a help to elevate and guide the mind, that it may be restrained from wandering from God. Besides, as the tongue was created above the other members, to celebrate the glory of God, it is proper that its whole power should be devoted to this service. And besides, the ardor of devotion sometimes impels the tongue, without our intention, to utter itself in an audible voice.

247 M. If it is so, what profit do those have who pray in an unknown language, without understanding it themselves?
C. That is nothing else, then trifling with God. Therefore, such hypocrisy should be removed from Christians.

248 M. But when we pray, shall we do it at a venture, uncertain of success or does it become us to be certainly persuaded that we shall be heard?
C. This should be the perpetual foundation of prayer that we shall be heard, and shall obtain whatsoever we ask, as far as is conducive to our good. For this reason, Paul teaches that a right invocation of God flows from Faith. For no one ever, in a right manner, called upon God, unless he first rested with a sure confidence upon his goodness.

249 M. What then is the case with those who pray doubtingly, and are uncertain, whether they shall obtain anything by prayer, or whether they shall be even heard of God?
C. Their prayers are vain and useless, as they are supported by no promise. For we are commanded to ask with an assured Faith, and the promise is added, that whatsoever we ask believing, we shall receive (Matthew 21:22; Mark 11:24; James 1:6; Psalm 1:15; 41:15; 145:18; Isaiah 30:19; 65:1;

Jeremiah 29:12; Joel 2:32; Romans 8:25; 10:13; 1 Timothy 2:5; 1 John 2:1; Hebrews 4:14; John 14:14).

250 M. But since we are, in so many respects, unworthy of his notice, how may we obtain this confidence that we should presume to place ourselves in his presence?
C. First, we have the promises, by which it is clearly determined, that the consideration of our own worthiness is omitted. Secondly, if we are sons, his Spirit will animate and awaken us, that we shall betake ourselves familiarly to him as to a Father. And although we are as worms of the dust, and pressed with the consciousness of our sins. Yet, that we may not dread his glorious majesty, he proposes to us Christ, the Mediator, as the way in which we may approach him, with the confidence, that we shall obtain his favor.

251 M. You understand, then, that God is not to be approached, but in the name of Christ alone?
C. So I think for he thus commands in express words, and the promise is added, that he will grant, through his intercession, that we shall obtain those things which we ask.

252 M. They are not then to be accused of rashness or arrogance who, relying on this Advocate, familiarly approach God, and propose him alone, both to God and themselves, as the way of acceptance?
C. By no means. He who thus prays offers his prayers, as from the mouth of his Advocate, knowing that his prayer is assisted and commended through his intercession (Romans 8:15, 33).

253 M. Let us now consider what the prayers of believers ought to contain. Is it lawful to request of God anything

which enters our mind, or is some certain rule to be observed?

C. It would be presumptuous, in prayer, to indulge our own inclinations and the will of the flesh. We are too ignorant to determine what is best for ourselves, and we labor under those irregular appetites which it is necessary should be restrained with a bridle.

254 M. What then must be done?

C. It is our privilege that God has prescribed for us the correct form of praying that we may follow him as if preceding our words, and guiding us by the hand.

253 M. What rule has he prescribed?

C. Ample and copious instruction on this subject is delivered to us in various parts of the scriptures. But that he might represent the object more clearly, he composed a formula, in which he has embraced and digested into a few heads, whatever it is lawful for us to ask of God, or that is for our benefit to obtain.

256 M. Rehearse it.

C. Our Lord Jesus Christ, being asked by his disciples in what manner they should pray, answered, when you pray, say: "Our Father, who art in Heaven, hallowed be thy name; thy kingdom come; thy will be done, on earth as it is in heaven. Give us this day, or daily bread; forgive us our debts, as we forgive our debtors; and lead us not into temptation; but deliver us from evil. For thine is the kingdom, the power, and the glory, forever, Amen" (Matthew 6:9; Luke 11:2).

257 M. That we may better understand what it contains, let us divide it into heads.

C. It contains six parts. The three first respect only the glory of God, as their peculiar object. The others respect us and our welfare.

258 M. Is anything then to be asked of God, from which no benefit is to be derived to ourselves?

C. He so orders all things from his infinite goodness, that whatever is for his glory is beneficial also to us. Therefore, when his name is sanctified, he causes it to turn to our sanctification. His kingdom cannot come, but that we are, in some manner, partakers of its privileges. But in praying for all these things, it is our duty, passing by all advantage to ourselves, to regard his glory alone.

259 M. Truly, according to this doctrine, these three petitions are also connected with our benefit. And yet we ought to aim at no other end, then this, that the name of God may be glorified.

C. It is so, and in like manner the glory of God is to be regarded by us, in the other three; although these are peculiarly designed for them who pray for those things which are for their own health and benefit.

260 M. Let us proceed now to an exposition of the words. And, first, why is the name Father, in preference to any other, here attributed to God?

C. As the first requisite of prayer is to have a firm assurance of conscience, God assumes this name to himself, which signifies nothing but pure kindness, so that our minds being freed from all anxiety, he invites us, familiarly, to approach him in prayer.

261 M. May we then confidently use that freedom in approaching God, which children commonly use in addressing their parents?

C. Yes, entirely and with a much surer confidence that we shall obtain what we ask. For, as our Lord teaches, if we, who are evil, cannot deny good things to our children, nor send them away empty, nor give them poison for bread, how much more beneficence is to be expected from our heavenly Father, who is not only the chief good, but goodness itself (Matthew 7:11)?

262 M. May we not, from this name also, draw an argument, to prove that which was said in the beginning, that all prayers ought to be founded on the intercession of Christ.

C. It does most assuredly. For God holds us in the place of children, only as we are the members of Christ (John 15:7; Romans 8:15).

263 M. Why do you call him our Father in common, rather than your own as an individual?

C. Every believer is able to call him his own, but our Lord used this common appellation, that he might accustom us to the exercise of charity in our prayers that no one should so much regard himself as to forget others.

264 M. What do you mean by that clause "who art in heaven?"

C. It is the same, as if I should call him, exalted, powerful, and incomprehensible.

265 M. Wherefore is it, and in what manner?

C. Truly, in this manner we are taught to raise our minds on high, when we pray to him, that our thoughts may not be occupied by earthly and carnal things that we may neither limit him by the measure of our understanding, nor by judging too meanly of him, be disposed to bring him into subjection to our wills. But that we may rather be taught to adore his glorious Majesty with fear and reverence. It tends also to awaken and confirm our confidence in him, while he is declared to be the Lord and ruler of heaven, ordering all things after the counsel of his own will.

266 M. What is the sum of the first petition?
C. By the name of God, the scriptures understand, that knowledge and glory of his which is celebrated among men. We pray therefore that his glory may be advanced everywhere and by all people.

267 M. But can anything be added to or taken from his glory?
C. In himself he is neither increased nor diminished. But we desire him to be made manifest according to his excellency among all people that whatever God does, that all his works, as they are, so they may appear to be, glorious; and that he may be glorified by all means.

268 M. What do you understand by the kingdom of God, in the second petition?
C. It consists chiefly in two things that he governs his elect, by his Spirit, and that he destroys the reprobate, who obstinately refuse to give up themselves in obedience to him that it may be manifest to all that there is nothing able to resist his power.

269 M. How do you pray that this kingdom may come?
C. That the Lord would daily increase the number of believers, that he would enrich them constantly with fresh gifts of his Spirit until they shall be perfected. Moreover, that he would render his truth more luminous, and his righteousness more manifest, by scattering the darkness of Satan, and abolishing all iniquity.

270 M. Do not all these things daily come to pass?
C. They so come to pass, that the kingdom of God may be said to be begun. We pray, therefore, that it may be continually increased and enlarged, until it shall be advanced to its highest glory which we trust will be accomplished at the last day when all creatures being reduced to subjection. God shall be exalted and shine forth and thus he shall be all in all (1 Corinthians 15:28).

271 M. What is the meaning of the petition "thy will be done?"
C. That all creatures maybe in submission to him and so depend on his pleasure that nothing may be done but by his will.

272 M. Do you suppose then that anything can be done contrary to his will?
C. We not only pray that what he has determined with himself may come to pass, but also that all obstinacy being subdued and subjected, he would bring the wills of all creatures into a harmonious obedience to his own.

273 M. By praying in this manner do we not give up our own wills?

C. Entirely. And not merely to this end that he would destroy in us, whatever desires are opposed to his will, but also that he would form our understandings and hearts anew, govern us by his Spirit, and direct our prayers, so that our wills may be in perfect agreement with his.

274 M. Why do you pray that his will may be done on earth as it is in heaven?
C. As the holy angels, who are his heavenly creatures, have but one purpose, to hear and obey his commands so I pray that men may have the same disposition of obedience, and that each one may devote himself to him in a willing subjection.

275 M. Let us now proceed to the second division. What do you understand by the daily bread which you ask?
C. In general, whatever conduces to the preservation of this present life not only food and raiment, but all those supports, by which the necessities of the body are supplied. And that we may eat our daily bread in quietness, as far as God shall judge to be expedient.

276 M. Why do you ask this to be given you of God, since he commands you to provide it by your own labor?
C. Although we must labor and sweat, for the purpose of preparing our daily food, yet we are not sustained by our labor, industry, and care but by the blessing of God alone, by which the labor of our hands is prospered, which otherwise would be in vain. Besides, it is to be considered that although he supplies abundance of food to our hands, and we feed upon it, yet we are not supported by its substance, but by the power of God alone. For these things have originally no virtue of this kind in themselves, but

their efficacy is of God, who from heaven administers it, through these as the organs of his bounty (Deuteronomy 8:3; Matthew 4:4).

277 M. But by what rule do you call it your bread, since you request it to be given you of God?
C. Truly, because it is made ours by the kindness of God, as it is by no means due to us. We are also admonished by this word, to refrain from seeking for ourselves, the bread of any other person, and to be contented with whatever comes to us, in a lawful way, as though it came to us immediately from the hand of God.

278 M. Why do you add "daily" and "this day"?
C. By these two particulars, we are instructed to use moderation and temperance lest our desires exceed the measure of our necessity.

279 M. But as this prayer is for the use of all persons, how can the rich, who abound in provisions laid up in their houses for a long time, ask their bread to be given them daily?
C. It is the duty of the rich and the poor alike, to hold this as settled that none of the things, which they possess, will profit only so far as God, by his favor, shall grant them the use, and make the use itself fruitful and effectual. Therefore, in possessing all things, we have nothing, only as we hourly receive from the hand of God, what is needful and enough.

280 M. What do you pray for in the fifth petition?
C. That the Lord would pardon our sins.

281 M. Is there no one to be found, of all men, who is so just, as not to need this forgiveness?

C. No, not one. For when Christ gave this form of prayer to his disciples, he appointed it for the whole Church. And therefore, he who would exempt himself from this petition, ought to depart from the society of believers. And we have the sure testimony of the scriptures, that he who would contend to justify himself in one point, before God, would be found guilty of a thousand others. This one thing therefore alone remains for all, to take refuge in his mercy (Hebrews 9:8).

282 M. In what manner do you consider our sins to be forgiven us?

C. According to the meaning of the words of Christ; that they arc debts, which hold us bound by the condemnation of eternal death, until God shall deliver us by his pure munificence.

283 M. You say then that we obtain the forgiveness of our sins by the abounding grace of God?

C. Entirely. For if the punishment of one sin, even the least, was to be redeemed, we could, by no means, make the satisfaction. It is necessary therefore, that all sins be gratuitously remitted and forgiven.

284 M. What benefit do we obtain by this remission?

C. Even this that we are made acceptable to him, as though we were innocent and righteous. At the same time, the confidence of his paternal benevolence is confirmed in our consciences, whence salvation is made sure to us.

285 M. What is the condition appointed, that he would forgive us, as we forgive our debtors? Does it mean, that by pardoning men their offenses against us, we ourselves merit pardon of God?

C. By no means for then it would not be a gratuitous remission. Nor would it be founded, as it ought, solely on the satisfaction of Christ, which he made for us on the cross. But by forgiving the injuries committed against us, we shall imitate the clemency and goodness of God, and prove by this that we are the children of God. By this rule, he would confirm us and at the same time, on the other hand, show us that unless we are ready and willing to forgive others, we can expect nothing else from him, but the highest and most inexorable rigor and severity.

286 M. This then you say, that all those, who will not, from the heart, forgive offenses, are rejected of God, and excluded from the adoption of children. Nor can they hope that there will be, in heaven, any forgiveness with God.

C. So I think that the saying may be fulfilled — the same measure which any one has measured out to others, shall be measured back to him again.

287 M. What is the next petition?

C. That the Lord would not lead us into temptation, but deliver us from evil.

288 M. Do you include the whole of this in one petition?

C. It must be one petition as the last clause is an explanation of the first.

289 M. What does it summarily contain?

C. That the Lord would not permit us to fall into sin, nor leave us to be overcome by the devil, nor by the lusts of our flesh which carry on an unceasing war with us. But that he would rather provide us with his power for resisting, sustain us by his hand, and defend and cover us with his shield, that so, under the confidence of his guardianship we may dwell in safety.

290 M. But how is that done?
C. When, by the influence of his Spirit, we are imbued, with such a love and desire of righteousness, that we overcome sin, the flesh, and the devil, and on the other hand, with such a hatred of sin, as separates us from the world, and retains us in holiness. For our victory is effected by the power of the Spirit.

291 M. Have all persons need of this assistance?
C. Yes, for the devil continually watches us and as a roaring lion goes about seeking whom he may devour. And we should at once consider how weak we are, nay, that we should be overcome at each moment, unless God prepared us for the warfare with his armor, and strengthened us by his hand.

292 M. What is the meaning of the word temptation?
C. The cunning and deceitfulness of Satan, with which he constantly attacks us, and would with ease entirely circumvent us, unless we were assisted by the help of God. For our understandings, from their native vanity, are exposed to his wiles. Our wills, from their depraved propensity to evil, would wholly yield to him.

293 M. But why do you pray, that God would not lead you into temptation, since it appears to be the work of Satan, and not of God?

C. God defends believers by his protection, that they may neither be ensnared with the wiles of Satan, nor overcome by sin. So those, whom he accounts worthy of punishment, he not only deprives of his grace, but also strikes with blindness, gives up to a reprobate mind, and delivers over to the power of Satan, that they may be entirely the servants of sin, and exposed to all the assaults of temptation.

294 M. What is the meaning of this conclusion — for thine is the kingdom, the power, and the glory forever?

C. By this we are again reminded, that our prayers are more strengthened, by his power and goodness, than by any confidence of our own. Besides, we are taught to close all our prayers with the praises of God.

295 M. Is it lawful to ask nothing of God, but what is comprehended in this formulary?

C. Although we have liberty to pray in other words, and in another manner, still however, it is to be considered, that no prayer can be pleasing to God, which is not referred to this, as the correct standard of the nature of prayer.

IV. OF THE WORD OF GOD

296 M. Now the proposed method of instruction requires of us, to treat of the fourth part, of the honor due to God.

C. We said that it consisted in this, that we acknowledge God to be the author of all good, and that we confess his goodness, justice, wisdom, and power, with praise and thanksgiving that the fullness and glory of all blessings may abide in him.

297 M. What rule has he prescribed for this duty?
C. Those praises of him, which are published in the scriptures, should be received as a rule for us.

298 M. Does not the Lord's Prayer contain something which applies to this duty?
C. Yes, when we pray that his name may he sanctified, we desire that his glory may be manifested in all his works, that his mercy may appear in pardoning sinners, or his justice in punishing them, and his faithfulness in fulfilling his promises to his people. Finally, that whatever of his works we behold, it may excite us to glorify him. This is truly to ascribe to him the praise of all blessings.

299 M. What shall we conclude from those things about which we have already treated?
C. That which the truth itself teaches and the same which I proposed at first that this is eternal life, to know the only true God, the Father, and Jesus Christ, whom he hath sent. To know him, I say, that we may render to him due honor and worship not only as he is our Lord, but also our Father and Savior, and in our turn that we are his sons and servants and therefore that we devote our life to the celebration of his glory (Job 17:3).

300 M. In what way shall we arrive at so great a good?
C. For this end God has left us his holy word. For his spiritual doctrine is as the door by which we enter his celestial kingdom.

301 M. Where must we seek this word?

C. In the Holy Scriptures, in which it is contained.

302 M. How must the word be used, that we may receive fruit from it?

C. We must embrace it with a firm persuasion of heart, as the very truth delivered to us from heaven. We must yield ourselves teachable, and submit our understandings and wills, in obedience to it. We must love it from the heart, that being engraved on our souls, it may take deep root and produce its fruits in our lives and when we are conformed to this rule, it will become our salvation, as it is appointed.

303 M. Are all these things put in our power?

C. Not one of them indeed. But it is of God alone, by the grace of his Holy Spirit, to effect in us all that I have mentioned.

304 M. But must we not give diligence, and strive with all earnestness, by reading, hearing, and meditating, that we may profit therein?

C. Yes, truly. Each one should not only daily exercise himself in private reading but also at the same time, with special attention, frequently hear sermons in public meetings, where the doctrine of salvation is explained.

305 M. You say then that it is not sufficient for anyone to read by himself at home but that all must assemble together, to hear the same doctrine?

C. It is a duty to assemble together, when the opportunity is given.

306 M. Can you prove this to me?

C. The will of God alone ought to satisfy us, abundantly, for proof. He commended this order to his Church, not that two or three only should observe it but that all should unitedly be subject to it. Besides, he declares this to be the only method for the edification and preservation of his Church. This therefore should be to us a holy and inviolable rule, that it is not lawful for anyone to assume to himself, to be wise above his master.

307 M. Is it then necessary that there should be pastors in the Churches?
C. Yes, and it is our duty to hear them, and to receive from their mouths, with fear and reverence, the doctrines of Christ which they publish. Those then who contemn them, or withdraw from hearing them, despise Christ, and make a division in the society of believers (Matthew 10:40).

308 M. Is it enough for a man, to have been once instructed by his pastor or ought this course to be pursued through life?
C. It is useless to begin, unless you persevere. For it becomes us to be the Disciples of Christ even unto the end, or rather without end. And he hath committed this office to the ministers of the Church that they should teach us in his name and stead.

V. OF THE SACRAMENTS

309 M. Are there other means, besides the word, by which God communicates himself to us?
C. Yes, to the preaching of the word, he has added the sacraments.

310 M. What is a sacrament?

C. It is an outward testimony of the divine benevolence towards us, which, by a visible sign, shadows forth spiritual graces, by which the promises of God are sealed in our hearts that the truth of them may be more firmly established.

311 M. Is there such great power in the visible sign, as to confirm our consciences in the confidence of salvation?

C. It has not indeed that efficacy of itself, but from the will of God, as it is instituted for this end.

312 M. Since it is the peculiar office of the Holy Spirit, to seal in our minds the promises of God, how do you attribute this to the sacraments?

C. The difference between the Spirit and these is very great. For it is truly the work of the Spirit alone to move and affect the heart, to illuminate the understanding, and to render the conscience stable and tranquil. That work ought to be accounted wholly his own, and acceptance should be referred to him, lest the praise be transferred elsewhere. But this by no means prevents, that God uses the sacraments as secondary organs, and applies those things in their use as seems him good. He so does it that nothing is derogated from the power of the Spirit.

313 M. You believe then, that the power and efficacy of the sacrament, do not consist in the external element, but that they proceed solely from the Spirit of God?

C. So I think. And truly it pleases the Lord to put forth his power, through his own institutions, for that end, for which he appointed them. And he does this in a manner, which detracts nothing from the power of his Spirit.

314 M. Can you give me a reason why he operates in this way?
C. Truly, in this manner, he consults our infirmity. If we were wholly spiritual, like the angels, then we should be able spiritually to discern both him and his graces. But as we are enclosed in this earthly body, we need figures or glasses, which, in some sensible manner, may exhibit the spiritual aspect of heavenly things which otherwise we should not be able to discern. At the same time, it is for our benefit that all our senses be exercised on the promises of God, that they may be more strongly confirmed to us.

315 M. If it is true, that the sacraments were instituted of God, to be helps of our infirmities, must not those be justly condemned of arrogance, who judge themselves to be sufficient without them, or who account them useless?
C Most certainly. And therefore, if any one abstain willfully from the use of them, as if he had no need of them, he despises Christ, spurns at his grace, and extinguishes the Spirit.

316 M. But what confidence or real security, for confirming our consciences, can be derived from the sacraments, which are used promiscuously by the good and the bad?
C. Although the gifts of God are, in the sacraments, offered to the wicked, yet they reduce them to nothing, as I may say, in so far as it respects themselves. Still however, they do not destroy the nature and power which the sacraments have in themselves.

317 M. How and when does the effect follow the use of the sacraments?
C. When we receive them by faith, seeking, in them, only Christ and his grace.

318 M. Why do you say that Christ is to be sought in them?
C. I do not understand, that he is inherent in the visible signs, so that we should seek salvation from them, or imagine any power of conferring grace to be affixed to them, or shut up in them. But the sign is rather to be considered as a help, by which we are directly conducted to Christ, seeking from him salvation and every durable blessing.

319 M. As faith is required, for the right use of the sacraments, how do you say, that they are given to us for the confirmation of faith that they may render us more certain of the promises of God?
C. It is by no means sufficient, that faith be once begun in us, unless it be continually nourished and increased daily, more and more. For this end the Lord instituted the sacraments, to nourish, strengthen, and increase our faith. And this Paul teaches, when he says that these avail for sealing the promises of God (Romans 4:11).

320 M. But is it not a proof of unbelief, if we have not an established faith in the promises of God, unless they are confirmed to us by other means?
C. This surely argues the weakness of faith, under which the children of God labor who still, on that account, do not cease to be believers, although as yet they are endowed with small and imperfect faith. For as long as we are conversant in this world, the remains of distrust always adhere to our

flesh, which we are no otherwise able to shake off, than by continually making progress to the end of life. It is the duty of every one therefore to make farther progress in faith.

321 M. How many sacraments are there in the Christian Church?
C. Two only, the use of which is common among all believers.

322 M. Which are they?
C. Baptism and the Holy Supper.

323 M. What is the resemblance or difference between them?
C. Baptism is the appropriate way of entrance into the Church. For in this we have the testimony, that we who were before strangers and foreigners are received into the family of God and numbered among his household. But the Supper witnesses that God, by nourishing our souls, shows himself a Father to us.

324 M. That the nature of each may more distinctly appear, let us treat them separately. First, what is the signification of Baptism?
C. It has two parts. First, it represents the forgiveness of sins. Secondly, the regeneration of the soul (Ephesians 5:26; Romans 6:4).

325 M. What resemblance has water with these things, that it should represent them?
C. Forgiveness of sins is indeed a species of washing, by which souls are cleansed from their defilement, even as the filth of the body is washed off with water.

326 M. But how does water represent regeneration?
C. In as much as the beginning of regeneration is the mortification of our nature, and its end, our becoming new creatures. So, by putting water on the head, the figure of death is represented. As we do not remain buried in the water, but enter it only for a moment, and come forth immediately as from a sepulcher, a resurrection to newness of life is typified.

327 M. Do you suppose the water is the laver of the soul?
C. By no means. It is unlawful to wrest this honor from the blood of Christ, which was shed for this end, that we being cleansed from all our spots, he might present us pure and undefiled before God. And we indeed receive the fruit of this cleansing, when the Holy Spirit sprinkles our consciences with his sacred blood. But we have the seal of this cleansing in the sacrament (1 Peter 1:19; 1 John 1:7).

328 M. Do you attribute anything to the water, only as it is a figure of cleansing?
C. I consider it to be a figure, but at the same time, it has the substance connected with it. For God, in promising us his gifts, does not deceive us. Therefore, as forgiveness of sins and newness of life are offered to us in baptism, so it is certain that they are received by us.

329 M. Has this grace its effect, promiscuously upon all?
C. Many indeed close up the way to it, by their corruption, and make it a vain thing to themselves so that believers only are partakers of this fruit. But that diminishes nothing from the nature of the sacrament.

330 M. Whence have we regeneration?
C. Both from the death and resurrection of Christ. For this power is in his death, that by it our old man is crucified, and the corruption of our nature is, in a manner, buried, so that it no more prevails in us. But it is the benefit of the resurrection, that we are begotten unto a new life, to the obedience of the righteousness of God.

331 M. How are these benefits conferred on us by baptism?
C. By this we are clothed with Christ, and endowed with his Spirit, unless by rejecting the promises, we render the benefits offered therein to us unfruitful.

332 M. What must we do, in order to use baptism in a right manner?
C. The right use of baptism is placed in faith and repentance. That is, that we first determine, by a sure confidence of soul, that we are cleansed from all spots by the blood of Christ, and are acceptable to God. Then that we believe that his Spirit dwells in us and that we make this manifest by our works among others. Also that we assiduously exercise ourselves in striving for the mortification of the flesh, and obedience to the will of God.

333 M. If these things are required for the legitimate use of baptism, how comes it to pass that we baptize infants?
C. It is not necessary, that faith and repentance always precede baptism. These are required only of those who from age are capable of both. It is sufficient, if infants, after they come of age, produce the fruits of their baptism.

334 M. Can you prove to me that there is nothing unreasonable in this?

C. Truly, I can, if it is conceded to me, that our Lord instituted nothing which is unreasonable. For although Moses and all the prophets teach, that circumcision was the sign of repentance, and Paul that it was the seal of the righteousness of faith. Yet, we see, that infants were not excluded from it (Deuteronomy 30:6; Jeremiah 4:4; Romans 4:11).

335 M. But are infants admitted to baptism now for the same reason that they were then admitted to circumcision?
C. Entirely the same. For the promises, which God gave to the people of Israel, are now published through the whole world.

336 M. Do you conclude from this that the sign is also to be used?
C. He who well examines the subject on both sides, will observe that this is the consequence. For Christ has not made us partakers of his grace, which was before given to Israel, by a measure, which should be to us rather more obscure, or in any part diminished. He has rather poured forth his grace upon us in a more clear and abundant manner.

337 M. Do you think, that if infants were excluded from baptism, they would, on that account, so lose any of the favor of God, as that it might be said, that their privileges were diminished by the coming of Christ?
C. That is indeed evidently manifest. For the sign being taken away—which availed so much in testifying the mercy, and confirming the promises of God—We should be deprived of that most excellent consolation, which the Church from the beginning enjoyed.

338 M. This is your opinion then — As much as God, under the Old Testament, that he might show himself to be the Father of little children, commanded the promise of salvation to be engraved on their bodies, by a visible sign, it would be a reproach, if believers, after the coming of Christ, should have a less confirmation. When the same promise, which was formerly given to the Fathers, is ordained for us in these days, when God exhibits to us in Christ a clearer manifestation of his goodness.

C. So I think. Besides, as it is sufficiently evident, that the power and substance (so to speak) of baptism, are common to infants, then if the sign is denied them, which is inferior to the substance, a manifest injury will be done them.

339 M. For what purpose then are infants baptized?

C. That they may have the visible seal. That they are the heirs of the blessings promised to the seed of believers, and that after they come to years of discretion, the substance of their baptism being acknowledged, they may, from it, receive and bring forth fruit.

340 M. Let us proceed to the Supper and in the first place, I would know of you what is its signification?

C. It was instituted by Christ, that by the communion of his body and blood, he might nourish our souls in the hope, and give us assurance of eternal life.

341 M. Why is the body of our Lord represented by bread and the blood by wine?

C. We are taught by this, that as bread has the power of nourishing our bodies, and of sustaining the present life so the same power is in the body of our Lord for the spiritual nourishment of our souls. And as with wine the hearts of men are cheered, their powers renewed, and the whole body strengthened, so from the blood of Christ, the same benefits are to be received by our souls.

342 M. Are we then fed by the body and blood of the Lord?
C. So I think. For as in this is placed our whole confidence of salvation, that the obedience which he has rendered to the Father should be imputed to us, and accounted as ours, so it is necessary that he should be received by us. For we are not otherwise made partakers of his benefits, but only as he makes himself ours.

343 M. But did he not then give himself to us, when he offered himself to death, that he might reconcile us, redeemed from the sentence of death, to the Father?
C. That is indeed true, but it is not sufficient for us, unless we now receive him, that we may partake of the fruit and efficacy of his death.

344 M. Does not the manner of our receiving Christ consist then in faith?
C. Yes, but I add this that it be done, while we not only believe that he died to deliver us from death, and rose again to procure life for us. But also that we acknowledge that he dwells in us, and that we are united to him, by that kind of union, by which the members are united to the head, so that, by the privilege of this union, we may be made partakers of all his benefits.

345 M. Do we obtain this communion through the Supper only?

C. By no means. For by the gospel, as Paul testifies, Christ is communicated to us, as we are therein taught, that we are flesh of his flesh, and bone of his bone, that he is the living bread, which came down from heaven to nourish our souls, and that we are one with him, even as he is one with the Father and such like things (1 Corinthians 1:6; Ephesians 5:30; John 6:51; 17:21).

346 M. What other benefit does the sacrament confer on us?
C. This — that the communion which I mentioned is strengthened and confirmed to us. For although both in baptism and the gospel, Christ is offered to us. Yet in these we receive him, only in part.

347 M. What have we then in the symbol of the bread?
C. The body of Christ. That as he was once offered a sacrifice for us, to reconcile us to God, so now he is to be given to us, that we may assuredly know that reconciliation belongs to us.

348 M. What have we in the symbol of the wine?
C. Christ poured out his blood once, in satisfaction for sins, and as the price of our redemption. So we believe, that it is now reached out to be drank by us, that we may receive its benefits.

349 M. According to these two answers, the Holy Supper of the Lord calls us back to his death that we may partake of its efficacy?
C. Yes, wholly. For at that time, one only and perpetual sacrifice was perfected; which might suffice for our salvation. Therefore nothing more remains for us, but to receive its fruits.

350 M. Was not the Supper then instituted for this end, that we should offer to God, the body of his Son?

C. By no means. For the prerogative of offering for sins belongs to Christ alone as he is the eternal Priest. And this is the meaning of his word when he says, "Take and eat." He does not here command us to offer his body but only that we should feed upon it (Hebrews 5:10; Matthew 26:29).

351 M. Why do we use two signs?

C. In this the Lord consults our infirmity, as he would teach us more familiarly, that he is not only the food for our souls, but also the drink that we may seek our spiritual life wholly in him alone.

352 M. Should all persons without exception equally use both?

C. So Christ commands and it is the highest impiety for anyone to derogate in any manner from that, by attempting anything different.

353 M. Have we in the Supper the sign only of those benefits, you mentioned or are they therein, in very deed, given to us?

C. As Christ our Lord is truth itself, it is not to be doubted at all, but that he fulfills to us, at the same time, those promises which he gives to us therein, and adds its substance to the figure. Wherefore I do not doubt, but that as he is witnessed by words and signs, so he will make us partakers of his substance, that we may be united with him in one life.

354 M. But how can this be done, since the body of Christ is in heaven, and we are still sojourners on earth?
C. He effects this by the marvelous and secret influence of his Spirit with whom it is easy to unite those things which are otherwise separated by a great distance of places.

355 M. You do not suppose then that the body of Christ is enclosed in the bread, or his blood in the cup?
C. By no means. But I think this, that in order to possess the substance of the signs, our minds must be raised to heaven, where Christ is, and from whence we look for him, the Judge and Redeemer. But it is wicked and useless to look for him in these earthly elements.

356 M. This we may sum up in one head the things which you have said. You assert that there are two things in the Supper, bread and wine, which are seen with the eyes, handled with the hands, and perceived by the taste. And finally that our souls spiritually feed upon Christ, as their own proper aliment.
C. Yes, truly and therein is the resurrection of our bodies also confirmed to us, as by a given pledge, as they are made partakers of the symbol of life.

357 M. But what is the true and lawful use of this sacrament?
C. Such as Paul defines it to be — let a man examine himself, and so let him eat of that bread and drink of that cup.

358 M. What should be the object of this examination?
C. Whether he is a true member of Christ.

359 M. By what evidence shall he know that he is a true member of Christ?
C. If he possesses true faith and repentance, if he exercises sincere love towards his neighbors, and if his mind is free from all hatred and malice.

360 M. But do you require in man perfect faith and charity?
C. Truly, it is necessary that both faith and charity be free from all hypocrisy. But among men no one will ever be found absolutely perfect. Therefore the Holy Supper would have been instituted in vain, if no one might partake of it who is not wholly perfect.

361 M. Should not the imperfection then, under which we here labor, prevent our coming to the Supper?
C. By no means, for if we were perfect, the Supper would have no further use among us, as it is appointed to be a help for relieving our weakness, and a refuge for our imperfection.

362 M. Have not these two sacraments some other proposed end?
C. They are also marks, and as it were tokens of our profession. For in the use of them we profess our faith among men, and testify that we have one mind in the religion of Christ.

363 M. If anyone should despise the use of these, in what estimation is he to be held?
C. This certainly would be judged to be an indirect denial or Christ. Certainly anyone, since he disdains to profess himself a Christian, is unworthy to be numbered among Christians.

364 M. Is it sufficient to have received each sacrament once in a whole life?

C. One baptism is indeed sufficient, and this cannot lawfully be repeated. But with regard to the Supper it is different.

365 M. What is that difference?

C. By baptism the Lord introduces and adopts us into his Church, and thenceforward considers us, as of his family. After he has written us in the number of his people, he testifies by the Supper, that he takes care of us, and nourishes us as his members.

366 M. Does the administration of baptism and the Supper alike appertain to all?

C. By no means. For these are the peculiar duties of those to whom is committed the public office of teaching — to feed the Church with the doctrine of salvation and to administer the sacraments are things united in a perpetual connection among themselves.

367 M. Are you able to prove that to me by the testimony of scripture?

C. Christ, indeed, gave the commission of baptizing expressly to the apostles. But in the celebration of the Supper, he commanded us to follow his example. And the Evangelists inform us, that he performed in that distribution the office of a public minister (Matthew 28:19; Luke 22:19).

368 M. But ought those pastors, to whom the dispensation of the sacraments is committed, generally to admit all persons without distinction?

C. As it respects baptism, since it is administered at the present day only to infants, all are to be admitted without distinction. But at the Supper, the minister ought to take care not to communicate it to anyone who is publicly known to be unworthy.

369 M. Why not?
C. Because it cannot be done without a contempt and profanation of the sacrament.

370 M. But did not Christ honor Judas, however impious, with the sacrament?
C. Yes, but his impiety was at that time secret. Although Christ himself knew it, still it was not as yet known to man.

371 M. What then shall be done with hypocrites?
C. The pastor has no power to reject them as unworthy. But he ought to wait till God so far reveals their iniquity, as that it becomes known to men.

372 M. What if he should know or be informed, that someone was unworthy?
C. That would by no means be sufficient for rejecting him from the communion, unless there be first had a legitimate trial and judgment of the Church.

373 M. It is important then to have a certain order of government established in the Churches?
C. It is true. Otherwise they can neither be well established nor correctly governed. And this is the order; that Elders be chosen who may preside in the *Censura morum*, or superintend the discipline of morals, and watch to correct small offenses, and who shall reject from the communion,

those whom they know to be without a capacity for receiving the Supper, and those who cannot be admitted without dishonoring God, and giving offense to the brethren.

ACKNOWLEDGEMENTS

Nearly every moment of editing this volume was done listening to the music of Gileah Taylor. Her album *Songs for Late at Night Vol. 2* lived up to its title on many occasions.

The encouragement from Shane Anderson and Trent Still was helpful as my original plans died a slow death. I must also thank Mathew B. Sims for formatting and cross-editing another hair-brain project.

Finally, I must thank my wife who proofread the catechism modernization.

ABOUT
JOSHUA TORREY

Joshua Torrey is a computer chip designer by day and by night writer/editor of Torrey Gazette. He lives with his wife Alaina and their children (Kenzie, Judah, and Olivia) in Austin, Texas. Together they serve their local body of Redeemer Presbyterian Church.

GRACE FOR SINNERS BOOKS

Visit GraceforSinners.com

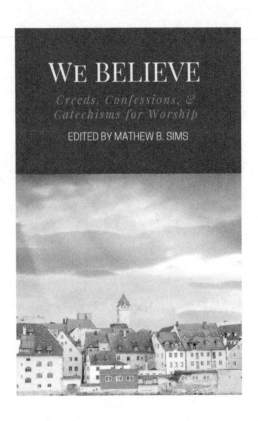

WE BELIEVE

*Creeds, Confessions, &
Catechisms for Worship*

EDITED BY MATHEW B. SIMS

In *We Believe: Creeds, Confessions, and Catechisms for Worship,* Mathew
has collected the essential church documents for Protestants: The Apostles'
Creed, the Nicene Creed, and the Athanasian Creed; the Dutch Reformed
Three Forms of Unity; the Westminster Confession and Shorter Catechism;
the London Baptist Confession and Spurgeon's A Puritan Catechism; the
Augsburg Confession and Luther's Small Catechism; and the Anglican's
Thirty-Nine Articles and an Outline of the Faith.

A HOUSEHOLD GOSPEL

FULFILLING THE
GREAT COMMISSION
IN OUR HOMES

MATHEW B. SIMS

In Scripture, parents are instructed to teach their kids how to love God and saturate their home with the gospel (Deut 4:9, 6:1-7; Eph 6:104). Husbands and wives are commanded to mirror Jesus in their marriages (Eph 5:22-33). We understand these commands in light of the gospel—in light of Jesus Christ (2 Cor 4:6). Jesus is the hero of our families.

That's what *A Household Gospel* is about. It's ordinary means rooted in an extraordinary gospel. It's about starting the great commission in our homes. It's about rehearsing the gospel story when we sit to eat, lay down to sleep, rise up in the morning, and everywhere in between.

Inside *Be Holy: Learning the Path of Sanctification*, Jason Garwood explores the terrain of sanctification in a comprehensive and easy to understand way. It's saturated in Scripture and rooted in the church's history of holiness—the ups and downs of growth and change in the Christian life. And at the center of *Be Holy* sits the reigning King Jesus and the work of the trinitarian God in the gospel. May God stir up your affections as you behold His glory and walk the path of sanctification.

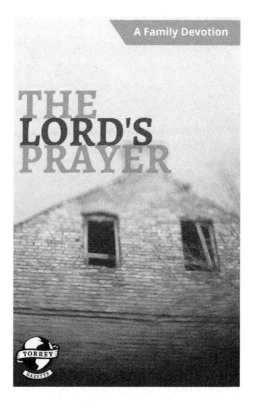

A Family Devotion

THE
LORD'S
PRAYER

TORREY
GAZETTE

Many modern definitions and practical guides on the subject of prayer are available today. Traditionally, prayer was taught through careful study of Christ's instruction on prayer. John Calvin who was at the center of the Reformation's return to biblical worship said, "No man will pray aright, unless his lips and heart shall be directed by the Heavenly Master."

In this vein, *The Lord's Prayer* delves deeply into the words of Christ to instruct families on the depth of riches available in this prayer. With guidance from the Psalms, the early church fathers, and the luminaries of the Reformation, The Lord's Prayer points to the singular truth of prayer—complete reliance upon God's promises.

Printed in Great Britain
by Amazon